Everyday *Quilts*

Your *Home* • Your *Style*

by marianne elizabeth

Everyday Quilts

Published by

All American Crafts, Inc.
7 Waterloo Road
Stanhope, NJ 07874
www.allamericancrafts.com

Publisher **Jerry Cohen**

Chief Executive Officer **Darren Cohen**

Product Development
Director **Brett Cohen**

Editor **Sue Harvey**

Art Director **Kelly Albertson**

Technical Illustrator **Rory Byra**

Photography **Van Zandbergen
Photography**

Product Development
Manager **Pamela Mostek**

Vice President/Quilting Advertising
& Marketing **Carol Newman**

Every effort has been made to ensure that the information presented is accurate. Since we have no control over physical conditions, individual skills, or chosen tools and products, the publisher disclaims any liability for injuries, losses, untoward results, or any other damages which may result from the use of the information in this book. Thoroughly read the instructions for all products used to complete the projects in this book, paying particular attention to all cautions and warnings shown for that product to ensure their proper and safe use.

Printed in China
©2010 All American Crafts, Inc
ISBN:978-0-9819762-5-9
Library of Congress Control
Number:2010936562

Dedication

To my husband, my college sweetheart, who keeps giving me more love and friendship than is imaginable.

To my son, whose cheerful disposition and inquisitive nature has never stopped searching for innovations and in doing so has been an inspiration to me.

To my parents, who showed us the world, and said you can be anything you want to be.

To my little girl ZsuZsu, my sweet Pekingese pup, who brought us great joy and playful happiness.

Acknowledgements

To Carol Newman, whose outstanding sense of humor and deep faith sees the best in each and every one.

This entire project would have remained wishful thinking or just a dream without the tireless help of Janet-Lee Santeusanio, the founder of Machine Quilters Exposition, who tirelessly, on broken heel/foot, turned the quilt tops into stunningly beautiful quilts.

To Pat Welch, whose perfect and speedy patchwork turned patterns into quilt tops and helped tamp down my panic when the deadlines drew nigh.

To Roberta Howson, who has supported my endeavors and quilting efforts for more than a decade with love, friendship and her expert quilting skills, contributing the piecing of a quilt top and its binding following shoulder surgery.

And to A Stitch In Time Quilters, Cathie & Michelle, who have proven to have exquisite machine quilting talents and through the years have helped immensely to create the Marianne Elizabeth Classically Home brand.

Thanks to One and All!

It's amazing what love and imagination can do!

marianne elizabeth

Contents

It's Your Home! Make It Your Style!

Decorate with Fabric

Create Your Style

It's Your *Home!*

*D*oes your family have its own set of special family traditions? Are there special ways and things you use to decorate throughout the year? Do you pull out a favorite quilt or decorate with treasured collectibles when celebrations occur? To me quilting is much more than the process and enjoyment of designing and sewing a quilt. Quilting is about creating something that becomes a part of your home and your life. A quilt becomes a part of family traditions and as familiar as the picture of Grandma and Grandpa on the wall. The pleasure of creating something that is well-used and cherished lasts far longer than the satisfaction of completing a project.

For my son, the little touches seemed to be the ones he noticed the most, and now that he's grown, they're the ones he looks for first when he comes home. When my son returned from college, the "sofa" quilt, soft through lots of cuddling, wasn't where it should have been. He immediately wanted to know where it had gone.

You might guess that as a fabric designer, I am the ultimate fabri-holic; I must say that while I enjoy many fabrics, I truly love those that "look like home." Creating fabrics that look like they belong in your room, match your sense of style, and coordinate with the decor and theme of your home requires looking beyond the "isn't this cute" and thinking in terms of "how would that look in my room?" That is what my fabrics are all about—giving the quilter a palette of fabrics that looks like home, to create rooms in which you love to live. After all, it's Your Home and it should be about Your Style.

Have you ever heard or used the phrase, "I got my money's worth"? A quilt that matches your decor is one you will use. It becomes one that you love sleeping under, or one that guests always admire hanging on the wall. It is one where the time, effort, and money invested was well worth it. My mom would say, "If you want it, I expect you to wear it. If you aren't going to wear it, take it back now. If I find it curled up in a ball in the corner of your drawer, unworn, you will hear from me loud and clear." To me that kind of economy applies to quilting; if you aren't going to use it in your home, if you wouldn't drape it on your sofa, if you won't hang it on the wall, then shouldn't you figure out why and correct whatever it is that makes it unsuitable?

It's that perspective that I use when creating and designing new fabrics for my fabric collections. I look for colors that are compatible with current color trends. If you make a quilt from them, will you find sheets and towels to match? Do the colors pop when the quilt is draped across your bed, brushing up against the headboard? And how are current design trends changing? While all of these elements will change over time, the one thing that is constant is that a well put-together room isn't just born. We've all walked into rooms that made us wish we were home. That kind of success is the result of paying attention to details, learning to discern what elements are needed to create "a look," and having the time and patience to pull them all together.

My fabric collections have focused on creating the perfect master or guest bedroom, the suite retreat. Why not have a "bed and breakfast experience" from the moment you open your eyes each morning to the last minute before you rest your head for the evening? We'll walk through the process of transforming a room with fabric, moving beyond the quilt with quick and easy coordinates that transform the look from nice to sensational, creating your own room makeover plan, and then talk about fabric selection. While you may just love what you see in these pages, what happens when the fabrics are gone or the colors just don't match your decor? And how do you find quilt designs and quilting fabrics that match a variety of decorating styles, whether traditional, country, coastal or contemporary?

Don't worry. You need not take on an entire room makeover unless you choose to. All of these processes and lessons will sharpen your design eye and work to improve the look of the project you undertake whether it is a single quilt or an entire ensemble. Use the parts of these lessons that apply to the project at hand, knowing that you can always return to this reference and revisit the sections that will help you solve the problems you are addressing that day.

Enjoy, and may all your quilts become truly loved,

marianne elizabeth

Decorating with Fabric

Are you bored with the decor of your bedroom? You feel as if you are stuck with the look since, after all, the only way to change it is to spend a lot of money buying new furniture. Not true! You can transform a tired look without an expensive investment in the purchase of new furniture or carpeting.

Imagine redecorating an entire room, completely changing its appearance, using nothing more than fabric, your creativity, and your sewing talents. If you've been quilting for even just a short time, you may know the thrill and excitement of dressing a bed in a new quilt and how it refreshes the look of a room.

Why stop with just the quilt? What can you do to go beyond the bed quilt to dress the entire room with coordinated fabrics, in a manner that enhances and completes the look established through the quilt's design and color palette?

While a pretty quilt can be lovely, it's really the addition of the ensemble extras that transforms the look from pretty to show stopping. Think about how much sense this makes. Picture an empty room. Just adding the furniture doesn't finish the room. It's the pictures, the throw rugs, the drapes, and all of the little things that pull it all together.

Dressing the bed begins

with sheets coordinated to match the quilt and décor. The next step in creating a polished look is to turn your attention to the pillows. Coordinated pillowcases and pillow shams, designed with the quilt's block pattern, frame the head of the bed and begin to pull the look together. These coordinates are quick projects that are easy to make in an afternoon, or squeeze in during an after-dinner sewing session.

A duvet or lap quilt thrown across the foot of the bed will go a long way to taking the chill out of even the coldest winter night, or provide a favorite place for pets to park while preventing the foot of the bed quilt from being soiled.

Quick and easy finishing touches can complete the look of a room and transform the bedroom into a dream retreat. Consider decorating a lampshade in one of the ensemble's accent fabrics. Drape a quilted runner on

the dresser or use a placemat-size quilt to protect a nightstand from scratches. Cover a small round decorator table with a floor length tablecloth and add a square table topper with accenting trim. Simple window treatments, such as valances or café curtains, add just the right finishing touch.

Take advantage of 108" wide goods, available in an array of colors and patterns, to create quick and easy duvets, table runners, or shower curtains. A 90" square hemmed on all sides makes a quick and easy topper for a 36" round decorator table.

The master bath provides another venue in which to expand the master suite project. Shower curtains, window curtains, vanity skirts, and tub surrounds are perfect places to splash with fabric. Fluffy towels become elegant accents when embellished with machine embroidery or trimmed with a coordinating ruffle.

Are you excited yet? Then close your eyes tight. Do you remember the last time you shopped for readymade home bedding and linens and took a good hard look at the quality, or the lack of quality, often found in commercially made products? Did it discourage you to see how poorly made many of the items are, no matter how big the brand label? Did you want more for your money like better construction, higher quality materials, colors more suited to your decor, and fabrics in colors you actually love? Then let's get started.

tart with a Plan

A professional decorator doesn't just waltz into a room, stack it with furniture and accessories from floor to ceiling, and declare the project complete. She begins by making a plan. The following is a simple planning process to organize the room transformation into easily accomplishable tasks that when completed will result in the redecoration of the room using fabric, your imagination, and simple sewing skills. This process can become just as much fun as the actual doing. Take your time and have fun along the way. Whether you are planning a quilt or a room makeover, using this framework will help you end up with a look that reflects your style.

Let's get to work. Prepare a notebook with blank paper and a pocket folder or an organizer to help keep all of the tidbits you'll be collecting together in one place. Be sure to take notes and jot down ideas as you work through the process.

The first thing you need to decide is what stays and what goes. Look at the room you'd like to refresh. Are you willing to change color schemes completely? What color is your carpet? What colors will coordinate with the existing decor? Do you need to stay with colors that will match the sheets and blankets you already own, or will it be ok to buy something new? Do you have wallpaper? Does it stay? Are you happy with the color of the paint in the room? A new coat of paint is a quick and inexpensive way to change the framework of your room's decor, while keeping to a low-cost budget makeover. In your notebook, make a list of the things that stay on one half of a sheet of paper. On the other half of the page make a list of what you'll be changing.

$\mathscr{S}et$ Your Style

Color and style are equally important in this process and set the mood that you are hoping to create through your selections and decorating process. Here is where pictures speak volumes. Begin by taking a very close look at room settings in books and magazines. Online retailers can be a great resource for this as well. Visit furniture manufacturers and retailers' websites, and search for retailers of other home decor items. Often these sites will have terrific room settings. Look for rooms you'd like to be relaxing in now! Print your favorite room settings and add them to your notebook.

When you are reviewing these pictures, consider the mood of the room. Is it formal and serious? Is it casual and playful? Is it warm and inviting or cool and clutter free? Does it look like the great outdoors, a rustic cabin, a New York metro chic apartment, or a romantic country inn? You'll begin to see how different color choices and fabric selections impact the look created. Take note of how the styles of furniture in the room work with the theme of the decor and how many elements combine to create one look. Are the lines of the furniture curved and ornate? Do the accessories repeat the look of the curved lines and accents, such as picture frames and fabrics, emphasize the ornate style?

Brighter colors and large splashy prints spell contemporary and modern. The furniture in these settings is often plain with simple, straight and clean lines. Cool colors are often used in an urban chic setting with tones of gray, hues of purple, and the use of black and white as the backdrop of very modern designs. Geometric prints, solid colors, fabrics with little detailing and those with large graphic shapes support the mood of this style.

Gather a selection of rooms or bed ensemble photographs that are most similar to the look you'd like to achieve. Try to narrow it down to one or two photos that are the most complete, showing not only the stylestyle (traditional, contemporary, formal, casual, etc.), but also the color scheme for the room or quilt project you'll be tackling.

Create a Palette

Once you have made decisions about the core elements in your room that will remain intact, the next step is to start envisioning what color you would like the room or quilt project to feature as its primary color and what its accent color might be. Perhaps you are continuing with an existing color. Not to worry, changing its dominant accent can change the look and yield a color scheme that makes the room feel new again.

If your core color is not changing, one way of giving the room a different look is to change values. Do you use mostly dark tones now? Lighten it up! Are your colors on the pale side? Choose some rich dark shades. Changing the style of print can also change the look considerably even while remaining within the same color family. For example, an oversized paisley or damask creates a vastly different look from that of small-scale plaids and checks. Another way to create a new look without changing the dominant color—find a new accent color and use it lavishly. It will become the drama point for the room and the primary color will work as a background color.

Even if you are working with a room that features neutral colors and your existing palette is a virtual clean slate, there are still some things to consider when picking a new color scheme. The overall tone of the woodwork in the room, including any wood flooring, moldings, and window frames, sets a backdrop that cannot be ignored when choosing a new color scheme. The wood floors in the room, for example, might feature a warm, natural oak with very warm, yellow-red base tones. A very cool, grayed color palette might look icy and harsh, especially at points where

the two color families meet, such as where the walls meet the floor. While we tend to think of wood floors as neutral, they do set the stage and the colors used in the room need to be compatible.

The color of the furniture in the room is the next major backdrop against which all essential elements of the room's decor must blend. Is the furniture white or off-white? Consider a fresh blue or red and white color scheme. Is the tone deep and dark, such as the sleek black so widely featured in furniture stores? Look for colors that will support the deep dark tones, but still have enough richness and depth to sparkle against the dark backdrop.

As you start to consider the colors you will use in the room, try to pull together as many samples as possible. Gather paint chips, fabrics from your stash, household items, flowers, leaves, or anything and everything that is small and moveable that represents the color palette. You'll want to take a closer look at the colors in your palette with a critical eye to see if they

really create the mood that you are seeking. Review the colors at different times of day, in various lighting conditions. Most colors sparkle on a sunny day, but some look especially drab on a dark cloudy day.

Using painter's tape, adhere the paint chips to the wall at eye level and leave them up on the wall. It's best to develop your palette over a period of time rather than make the decision in one day. We've all bought something we thought looked terrific only to later rue the day, deciding it really wasn't a great color, or a great fit, or a great look. While you are auditioning colors, it is easy to take risks and try unexpected combinations. Maybe you are staying with the same main color and only bringing in a new accent color. Maybe you are going for an entirely new color scheme. In either case, try colors you wouldn't normally choose. Refer to the room setting photos you've gathered.

If you need help choosing a color scheme, and your searches through magazines have not inspired you with just the right one, consider looking for color combinations in a paint store. Many times there will be small clusters of coordinating chips that have been grouped by the company's color experts into palettes that work well together. These often have a focal color as well as the perfect accent tones. Use a color wheel and become familiar with various types of color schemes.

Once you have picked a palette and determined what you want as accent colors, create a master palette with paint chips that best represent the look of the room or the quilt project. Don't worry, you're still playing with fabric, paper and snips from your stash. Nothing is set in stone and as you proceed, you can make changes if you find your selections need modification. Don't forget to include chips in your palette to represent the colors of the flooring, woodwork, furniture and walls. These elements represent your "baseline" colors and the backdrop for the entire project.

Select a Quilt Design

Whether you are choosing fabrics for a quilt or studying how a room's look was created through the choice of the fabrics selected, the details that require attention are the same. If the goal is to create a quilt that matches the decor, doesn't the quilt's design have to be consistent with the room's decor? Absolutely! You will notice in the photos throughout this book that I've matched each quilt to a different bedroom collection, showing different decor styles from coastal to traditional. Not all quilts are country fresh!

Here are a few examples of pairing the right quilt design to match the fashion of the decor. With thousands of quilt blocks and patterns to choose from, these examples are not all inclusive. When choosing a block or quilt pattern to make, consider how it matches the framework of the style you're creating.

For contemporary decor, choose quilt designs that feature fewer pieces, large or oversized pieces, and simpler shapes. Rectangles, squares, and circles are consistent with this style. Avoid small pieces and lots of triangles.

For traditional decor, consider quilt designs that are appliquéd or choose pieced patterns with tradi-

tional block designs. Formal designs and intricate settings are typical. Two-color quilts such as red and white or blue and white also successfully translate into a traditional look.

For country decor, select quilts that feature very traditional patterns such as log cabin or basket blocks, or whimsical folk-art appliqué. The country look often includes borderless quilt designs or scrappy quilts without a dominant fabric.

Understand
Fabric Styles

The quilt's pattern or design is just one element of the quilt. The choice of fabrics completes and establishes the appearance of the project. Over time, I have developed a Palette Master System that I use in creating new fabrics. Here are fabric styles or categories of printed designs you will typically find in my collections:

Large Scale Floral: Used as the focal fabric of the quilt design, this print conveys the mood and sets the style for the project, as well as for the fabric collection. The colors in this fabric create the entire palette for the colorway.

Quilters often lament that large floral prints are too beautiful to cut. In my patterns I showcase their use in a variety of ways and strive to show that the prints can be quite effective when cut up and used in a surprising array of functions. I've used them in the border, in setting blocks, as block centers, as sashing, as binding, and as a narrow inner border. Sometimes it's just fun to cut it up in various sizes just to see how drastically different it looks. Of course, if you don't want to do this with your actual fabric, a color copy will work just as well for this design exercise. While I sometimes repeat the print throughout the quilt, other times I use it in just one way and allow it to become a coordinate, rather than the focal fabric, in that particular project.

Border Stripe: A border stripe can be used in many ways beyond the edges of the border. Narrow stripes in the design can be fussy cut to create sashing that acts to set the stage for a dynamic quilt layout. Create a simple and quick pillow using a showy border stripe.

Damask: Damask fabrics were originally woven fabrics made of silk and originated in China, dating back to the earliest centuries. These gave rise to woven linens, wools, and synthetic fibers in which the very process of weaving resulted in elaborate designs. In the last several hundred years, these were typically used in napkins, tablecloths, draperies, and upholstery, and were woven to achieve a tone-on-tone effect. The motifs often feature floral or botanical elements or other types of ornamentation such as fleur-de-lis and crests.

   In the quilting world, cotton damask designs have become an important part of the design palette. While they don't have the shiny, reversible, or raised feel of their woven counterparts, they do introduce a beautiful style of pattern used for its tonal qualities. Typically in medium and large scales, the designs are often directional, and highly detailed. Occasionally I have included multicolored damasks to add extra design interest into a collection.

Small- or Medium-Scale Floral: Occasionally the focal fabric of a collection, a small- or medium-scale floral is more typically a companion print to the larger, more dramatic design of the fabric collection. This design may be directional and may feature the same background color as the large scale floral or use one that is a coordinating accent color. This type of fabric works well cut up in pieced blocks or as binding.

Tossed Floral: Imagine taking a bunch of small rosebuds and tossing them up in the air and finding that they magically fall to the ground in an equally distributed manner. This is the feel of a tossed floral. It can be printed on the same color background as the focal floral in a collection or on a coordinating accent color. Because of the symmetry of its design and its very small scale, it is best used in a supportive role, such as pieces of a block, as a cornerstone, as binding, etc.

Geometrics: Dots, diamonds, ovals, circles, square-in-a-square, and other lineal based shapes comprise this category. Depending on the color, value, and scale of these motifs, they can work as a coordinating print, a background, or the focal motif.

Stripes: Stripes are designs containing lines or bands of color in varying widths often separating areas of ornamentation. These lines may be closely and evenly spaced or divide the fabric into narrower and wider sections. Often used in borders or on the bias as binding, stripes are used in home decor projects, such as pillows, to create strong accents.

Paisley: Originating in India, this design spread to Scotland when British soldiers brought home cashmere shawls. From roughly 1800 to 1850, the women of the town of Paisley, Scotland, adapted the design and wove woolen shawls; henceforth the design became known as paisley. The fundamental shape is like a teardrop, rounded at one end with a curving point at the other. Generally the inside of the teardrop shape contains abstract designs, many of Indian, Turkish or Asian origin. A large, densely packed style of paisley was popular in the 1870s and 1880s and became known as Turkish Paisley. Paisley can be small-scale and simplistic or extremely large, ornate, and densely packed, making it especially well suited for kaleidoscope quilt designs.

Depending on the particular paisley print in question, the fabric can work in different ways in relation to the other fabrics in a design. This makes it one of the most interesting and versatile print categories. Paisley prints can be very modern or very traditional and even satisfy the demands of the reproduction quilt enthusiast. Whether a focal print, a background, or a coordinate, the versatility of paisley designs and the wide range of motifs make it an ever popular collectible.

Toile: The name of this style of fabric comes from "Toile de Jouy," which originated in the village of Jouy-en-Josas near Paris. It refers to a cotton fabric printed with a repeat pattern of rural French country scenes from the 18th and 19th centuries. Traditionally the motifs were printed in navy, cranberry or black, but occasionally were executed in green, brown or magenta.

Toile is most associated with fabrics, curtains and upholstery in particular, though it has also been used for wallpaper and china. From time to time courageous designers experiment with using toile-patterned items for apparel. In the quilting market, toile prints are often reduced in scale and the motifs carefully selected to showcase the more romantic, botanical motifs. In some of my collections, as seen in home decor fabrics, I chose to set the toile on a colored background, giving new life to this wonderful genre. This style of fabric, depending on the particular coloration of any one print, can work as a focal print and be featured in the border and alternating blocks, become a fabulous background, or, as in the Mirabelle quilt, work in all three places.

Tonal or Tone-on-Tone: In the art world, a painter might try to execute a value scale in which the tints and shades of one color, starting with white or the lightest tint on one end, gradually change into the darkest shade or black on the other. In the quilting world, fabric designers have experimented with creating fabrics that offer a solid color palette while featuring subtle patterns created through the change of values. Marbled fabrics offer the quilter the opportunity to use something that introduces more interest than a solid color would because the subtle changes in value and color add depth and reduce the flat appearance of the cloth. When there is no identifiable design to the cloth, other than the shading, it is referred to as a tonal or tonal print.

Textured Tonal: Similar in coloration to a tonal, a textured tonal has the same subtle gradations of color but integrated into the design are simple, identifiable shapes such as swirls, flowers, leaves or other design elements. While technically some would argue that these really are truly nothing more than tonal prints and don't deserve any distinction between the two, I disagree. When I use the label Textured Tonal in the patterns, you should choose a print that has more design interest than does just a marble or shaded solid. Again, it is all about creating a variety of designs that work harmoniously together and getting the most you can out of each position in the quilt.

Basic: I define a basic as a very small-scale pattern, which is sometimes executed in shades of the same color. Typically the design element has an allover pattern that is nondirectional, although some designs may be directional. Often featuring shades of neutrals on white or off-white, a basic may contain more than one color, such as black on red or navy on cream.

$\mathcal{P}ut$ It Together

If you've worked through the process, you have a notebook full of inspiration, packed with visuals that reflect your style and the way you wish to translate it into a new room or a new quilt ensemble. You're almost ready to pick your projects, buy fabrics, and start sewing!

Prepare a master palette worksheet that summarizes everything you've gathered. Show a combination of coordinating color chips. Define the color values for the look you are seeking. What are the primary and coordinating colors? Are the colors light, medium or dark? Are the colors of equal value, or is there a high degree of contrast?

Define the fabric styles, and make a detailed list. Are the fabrics all the same scale? Is one a larger pattern? Are they equally dense? By this I mean do the patterns have the same amount of design, or are some very plain, and others very detailed or busy? Describe each fabric's design style or category along with its color value and print density. For example:

- Large-scale floral, densely packed flowers, in dark, bright shades on a rich, dark ground
- Small-scale paisley, loosely spaced, in subtle, soft tints, with minimal amount of color contrast
- Medium-scale damask, medium bright coloration with lots of tints and shades

The more detailed your eye becomes, the more closely you will understand the elements that were used to create the look you loved, and the one you are trying to mimic.

Choose a project suited to both the color palette and fabric styles you've selected. Here is the same quilt design, sewn in two different colorways. Notice that it creates two very different moods!

The final look you achieve is created from combining different elements—color, fabric design, and style. How do you translate that into selecting fabrics for a quilt? Do you pick a pattern to suit the fabrics or pick

fabrics that are best suited to the quilt design selected? You must consider both aspects together.

Often I meet people who have chosen a pattern and are on the hunt for fabrics to use in the pattern. Sometimes people pick a fabric and try to fit it into the pattern in ways that just don't effectively showcase the print. An example of this is using a small-scale print in place of a large-scale motif. Understanding the impact of these kinds of changes is key to selecting fabrics successfully. If your goal is to create a quilt with a completely different look, then be sure that you understand how the prints you want to use work to create your hoped-for look.

Here is an easy rule of thumb to match the impact of the original quilt: replace a fabric in the design with the same fabric style. Replace a tonal with a tonal. Replace a texture with a texture. Replace a paisley with a paisley or another fabric that has an equivalent amount of movement and density of design.

As you develop your critical eye and pay attention to the details that create what you behold, you will have a clearer vision of what your finished project will look like and ultimately be much more pleased with the results you achieve.

Time to Shop

With your notebook and worksheet in hand, it's finally time to go shopping! With a vision of what look you will be creating, you are finally ready to buy fabrics for your project. If you are tempted to stray from your plan, just consider how this change will impact your overall look and whether it will add to the style you are building through color, pattern, and design. And remember: It's Your Home! Make it Your Style!

Tuscany Terrace

Play up the drama with this stunning black quilt. This quilt features a sensational sashing design that serves to focus the eye and enhance the drama created by the alternating pieced and plain blocks. If black isn't your color, don't worry! This is a design that showcases a focal fabric. Repeating the focal fabric in the center of the pieced block, the alternate block and as a narrow outer border helps to tie the whole design together in a sleek but classic look that captures the essence of modern traditional.

Fabric & Supply Requirements

	Quilt	Alternate	Shams (2)
• Pale yellow geometric	1½ yards	1½ yards	----
• Light green textured tonal	4½ yards	4½ yards	½ yard
• Dark green textured tonal	1 yard	1 yard	⅓ yard
• Cream paisley print	1 yard	1 yard	¼ yard
• Purple damask	1 yard	1 yard	----
• Black floral	5 yards	5 yards	1⅞ yards
• Black rosebud print	2¼ yards	2¼ yards	¼ yard
• Plum geometric	2¾ yards	2¾ yards	½ yard
• Floral border stripe	----	----	⅝ yard
• Backing & Batting	114" x 130"	123" x 134"	----

- Sewing thread in colors to match fabrics
- Quilting thread in colors to match fabrics
- 2 queen pillows for shams
- Basic sewing supplies & rotary cutting tools

If you prewash your fabrics, there may be shrinkage. Adjust the yardages accordingly.

Finished Quilt Size: 105¼" x 121½" (Alternate Size: 114¾" x 125½")
Finished Sham Size: 30⅛" x 20⅛"
Finished Block Sizes: 10" and 6"
Skill Level: Intermediate

The difference between the sample quilt and alternative size is the width of the outer border. The extra width accommodates tall, pillow-top king mattresses.

STEP ONE:
CUTTING DIRECTIONS

Note: Please read all directions before cutting fabric. WOF = Width of fabric from selvage to selvage, approximately 42". Label the pieces with the letters given in the cutting steps. Cutting differences for the alternate size are shown in green.

From the pale yellow geometric, cut:
- (23) strips 2" x WOF; recut (92) 2" x 10½" O strips

From the light green textured tonal, cut:
- (8) strips 2½" x WOF; recut (128) 2½" G squares
- (10) strips 2⅞" x WOF; recut (128) 2⅞" squares. Cut each square diagonally in half once to make (256) D triangles.
- (2) strips 6½" x 104" lengthwise, parallel to the selvage edge for the third side borders
- (2) strips 6½" x 87¾" length-wise, parallel to the selvage edge for the third top and bottom borders

- Shams: (1) strip 2⅞" x WOF; recut (8) 2⅞" squares. Cut each square diagonally in half once to make (16) D triangles.

- Shams: (1) strip 2½" x WOF; recut into (8) 2½" G squares
- Shams: (4) strips 1½" x WOF; recut into (8) 1½" x 14⅝" W strips

From the dark green textured tonal, cut:
- (8) strips 2½" x WOF for C
- (1) strip 3½" x WOF; recut (4) 3½" H squares.
- (2) strips 2" x WOF; recut (24) 2" P squares
- (1) strip 2" x WOF; recut (4) 2" x 10½" L strips

- Shams: (1) strip 2½" x WOF; recut (8) 2½" C squares
- Shams: (2) strips 2¼" x WOF; recut (4) 2¼" x 16⅝" X strips

From the cream paisley print, cut:
- (8) strips 2½" x WOF for A
- (1) strip 2" x WOF; recut (16) 2" K squares
- (1) strip 4¼" x WOF; recut (4) 4¼" squares. Cut each square diagonally in half twice to make (16) J triangles

- Shams: (1) strip 2½" x WOF; recut (8) 2½" A squares

From the purple damask, cut:
- (2) strips 2" x WOF; recut (25) 2" M squares
- (1) strip 3⅜" x WOF; recut (6) 3⅜" squares. Cut each square diagonally in half twice to make (24) R triangles; discard (2) triangles.
- (9) strips 2" x WOF for the first border

From the black floral, cut:
- (2) strips 2½" x WOF for B
- (5) strips 10½" x WOF; recut 18) 10½" Q squares
- (2) strips 3½" x 116" (8¼" x 116") lengthwise, parallel to the selvage edge for the outer side borders
- (2) strips 3½" x 105¾" (5½" x 115¼") lengthwise, parallel to the selvage edge for the outer top and bottom borders

- Shams: (4) strips 2½" x WOF; recut into (4) 2½" x 24 5/8" Z strips and (2) 2½" B squares
- Shams: (2) strips 3½" x WOF; recut into (4) 2 ½" x 20⅝" ZZ strips

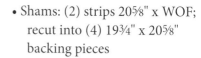

- Shams: (2) strips 20⅝" x WOF; recut into (4) 19¾" x 20⅝" backing pieces

From the black rosebud print, cut:
- (8) strips 2½" x WOF; recut (128) 2½" F squares
- (10) strips 2" x WOF for the second border
- (12) strips 2½" x WOF for binding

- Shams: (1) strip 2½" x WOF; recut (8) 2½" F squares

From the plum geometric, cut:
- 1 strip 2" x WOF; recut (4) 2" M1 squares
- (10) strips 2⅞" x WOF; recut (128) 2⅞" squares. Cut each square diagonally in half once to make (256) E triangles.
- (1) strip 2⅜" x WOF; recut (16) 2⅜" squares. Cut each square diagonally in half once to make (32) I triangles.
- (6) strips 2" x WOF; recut (24) 2" x 10½" N strips
- (3) strips 15⅜" x WOF; recut (5) 15⅜" S squares and (2) 8" x 8" T squares. Cut each S square diagonally in half twice to make (20) S triangles; discard (2) triangles. Cut each T square diagonally in half once to make (4) T triangles.

- Shams: (1) strip 8" x WOF; recut (4) 8" T squares and (8) 1½" V squares. Cut each T square diagonally in half once to make (8) T triangles.
- Shams: (1) strip 2⅞" x WOF; recut into (8) 2⅞" E squares. Cut each square diagonally in half once to make (16) E triangles.

From the floral border stripe, cut:
- Shams: (4) Y strips 2¾" x 16⅝" lengthwise, parallel to the selvage edge, with the border motif centered in each strip

STEP TWO:
PIECING THE QUILT TOP

Note: Use a 1/4" seam allowance throughout. Sew all pieces with right sides together and raw edges even, using matching thread. Press seams toward the darker fabric unless otherwise noted.

Sewing the Sister's Choice Blocks:

1. Sew a black floral B strip lengthwise between two cream paisley A strips. Repeat to make a second strip set. Crosscut the strip sets into (32) 2½" AB units.

2. Sew a cream paisley A strip lengthwise between 2 dark green C strips. Repeat to make four strip sets total. Crosscut the strip sets into (64) 2½" AC units.

3. Sew an AB unit between two AC units to make a Nine-Patch center. Press seams toward the A-C units. Repeat to make a total of 32 centers.

Make 32

4. To make one Sister's Choice block, sew a light green D triangle to a plum E triangle. Repeat to make a total of eight triangle units. Sew a triangle unit to two opposite sides of 4 black rosebud F squares to make side units.

Make 4

5. Sew a side unit to two opposite sides of a Nine-Patch center. Press seams toward the center. Sew a light green G square to each end of the 2 remaining side units. Press seams toward the G squares. Sew the strips to the top and bottom of the center to complete one 10½" x 10½" block.

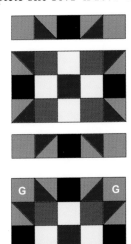

Make 32

6. Repeat steps 4 and 5 to complete a total of 32 Sister's Choice blocks.

Sewing the Variable Star Blocks:

1. Sew a plum I triangle to the angled edges of each cream paisley J triangle to make 16 side units.

Make 16

2. Sew a side unit to two opposite sides of each dark green H square. Press seams toward the H squares. Sew a cream paisley K square to each end of the remaining side units. Press seams toward the K squares. Sew a strip to the top and bottom of each H square to complete four 6½" x 6½" Variable Star blocks.

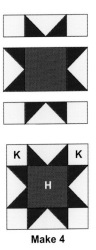

Make 4

Assembling the Quilt Top:
Note: Refer to the Quilt Assembly Diagram throughout the following steps. Press all border strips away from the quilt center.

1. Arrange the blocks in diagonal rows with the black floral Q squares, plum S triangles, pale yellow O strips, plum N strips and dark green L strips. Take a moment to study the Quilt Diagram to be sure the sashing strips are placed correctly.

2. Join the blocks and pieces together in diagonal block rows, alternating the Sister's Choice blocks with the black floral Q squares and separating each block, square and S triangle with L, N and O sashing strips. Carefully follow the Quilt Diagram to choose the correct positioning for each color sashing strip. Press all seams toward the sashing strips.

3. Sew the L, N and O strips together with the M and P squares and the R triangles to make sashing rows. Press all seams toward the L, N and O strips.

Hint

Make a photocopy of the quilt diagram and mark off each row as you complete it to be sure you are placing the correct sashing strip between each block, square and triangle. Place each row back into position as it is completed.

4. Sew the block rows together with the sashing rows, carefully matching all seams. Press each seam as you sew. Sew a T triangle to all four corners. Press the quilt top cen-

ter again. Carefully trim the quilt top all the way around, leaving a ¼" seam allowance beyond the block corners, to complete the 81¾" x 98" quilt center.

5. Sew the purple damask 2" x WOF strips short ends together to make one long strip. Cut two 81¾" strips and two 98" strips. Sew the longer strips to the long sides of the quilt center. Sew a plum M1 square to each end of the 81¾" strips. Press seams toward the strips. Sew the pieced strips to the top and bottom of the quilt center.

6. Sew the black rosebud 2" x WOF strips short ends together to make one long strip. Cut two 101" strips and two 87¾" strips. Sew the longer strips to the long sides and the shorter strips to the top and bottom of the quilt center.

7. Sew the light green 6½" x 87¾" strips to the top and bottom edges of the quilt center. Sew a Variable Star block to each end of the 6½" x 104" light green strips. Press seams toward the strips. Sew to the long sides of the quilt center, matching seams.

8. Sew the black floral 3½" x 116" (8¼" x 116") strips to the long sides and the 3 1/2" x 105 3/4" (5½" x 115¼") strips to the top and bottom to complete the quilt top.

STEP THREE:
QUILTING & FINISHING

1. Layer the backing right side down, batting and quilt top right side up. Baste the layers of the quilt together and quilt as desired.

2. Trim the backing and batting even with the quilt top.

3. Sew the short ends of the 2½" x WOF black rosebud print binding strips together into one long strip. Press the strip in half lengthwise with wrong sides together. Pin the raw edges of the binding even with the raw edges of the quilt. Sew the binding to the top with a scant ¼" seam allowance. Join the ends of the binding carefully. Turn the binding to the back and hand stitch it in place with matching thread and small, nearly invisible stitches.

Quilt Assembly Diagram

STEP FOUR:
COMPLETING THE SHAMS

Note: *Press all seams away from the sham center. Refer to the Sham Assembly Diagram throughout the following steps.*

1. Sew a black floral B square between two cream paisley A squares. Press seams toward the B square. Repeat to make a second AB strip. Sew a cream paisley A square between two dark green C squares. Press seams toward the C squares. Repeat to make a total of four AC strips.

A B A	C A C
Make 2	**Make 4**

2. Repeat steps 3–5 of Sewing the Sister's Choice Blocks to complete two blocks.

3. Sew a plum T triangle to each side of each block to make the sham centers. Press seams toward the triangles.

4. Sew a light green W strip to two opposite sides of each sham center. Sew a plum V square to each end of the remaining W strips. Press seams toward the strips. Sew the pieced strips to the top and bottom of the sham center.

5. Sew a dark green X strip to two opposite sides of the sham center. Repeat with the floral border stripe Y strips.

6. Sew the 2½" x 24⅝" Z black floral strips to the top and bottom and the 3½" x 20⅝" ZZ strips to the sides of the sham centers to complete the 30⅝" x 20⅝" sham tops.

Hint

If you wish to quilt the sham, now is the time to do it. Layer a 39" x 29" piece of batting and muslin and quilt as desired.

7. Complete the shams referring to the instructions on page 27.

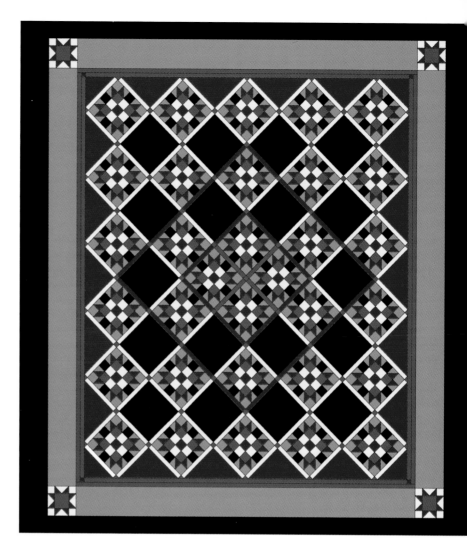

Alternate Quilt Assembly Diagram

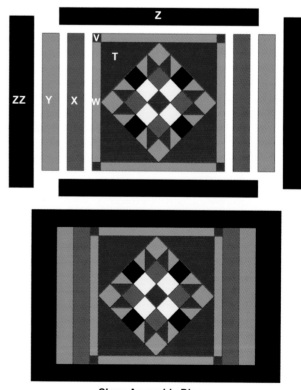

Sham Assembly Diagram

Pillow Sham Finishing

Use these basic instructions to complete any of the shams in this book.
The backing pieces were cut with the rest of the pieces in the quilt pattern.

1. Place two backing pieces right side up on a flat surface with the longer edges butted. ***Note:** The 19¾" edges of each backing piece are the top and bottom edges.*

2. Turn under the center edge of each piece ¾" and press. Turn under again 1¼" and press. Stitch along the inner folded edge to hem.

3. Place the sham tops right side up on a flat surface. Place a set of backing pieces right sides down on each sham top, overlapping the hemmed edges of the backing pieces to fit the tops.

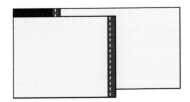

4. Pin the layers together to hold. Sew all around the outside edges with a ½" seam allowance.

5. Clip the corners close to the stitching line. Turn right side out through the back openings to complete the shams.

Briar Patch

Showcase fabulous floral fabrics or your favorite focus print with this pattern that allows that WOW print to be a star. Pull coordinating colors for the pieced block from your focal fabric and you've quickly got a successful color palette that will really allow that fabric you love room to bloom. Choose a coordinating border stripe for the outer border, or use your focus fabric for the outer border.

Fabric & Supply Requirements

	Quilt	Alternate
• Pale yellow geometric	1⅓ yards	1⅝ yards
• Light green textured tonal	1¼ yards	1¼ yards
• Dark green textured tonal	1½ yards	1⅔ yards
• Blue damask	1⅓ yards	1⅝ yards
• Ivory floral	2⅝ yards	3⅓ yards
• Floral border stripe	*7 yards	*7¼ yards
• Yellow tonal	1⅔ yards	1⅔ yards
• Blue floral tonal	1 yard	1 yard
• Backing & Batting	110" x 127"	127" x 127"
• Sewing thread in colors to match fabrics		
• Quilting thread in colors to match fabrics		
• Basic sewing supplies & rotary cutting tools		

*(4) 8" repeats will be cut from the width of the floral stripe. If your stripe will yield 4 cuts from one width of the fabric, you will need only 3¾ yards.

Finished Quilt Size: 101½" x 118½" (Alternate size 118½" x 118½")
Finished Block Size: 12" • **Skill Level:** Experienced Beginner

---

*If you prewash your fabrics, there may be shrinkage.
Adjust the yardages accordingly.*

STEP ONE:
CUTTING INSTRUCTIONS
Note: Please read all directions before cutting fabric. WOF = Width of fabric from selvage to selvage, approximately 42". Label the pieces with the letters given in the cutting steps. Cutting differences for the alternate size are shown in blue.

From the pale yellow geometric, cut:
• (17) (20) strips 2½" x WOF for A

From the light green textured tonal, cut:
• (14) (16) strips 2½" x WOF for C

From the dark green textured tonal, cut:
• (14) (16) strips 2½" x WOF for D
• (10) (10) strips 1¼" x WOF for the first border

From the blue damask, cut:
• (17) (20) strips 2½" x WOF for B

From the ivory floral, cut:
• (7) (9) strips 12½" x WOF; recut (20) (25) 12½" E squares

From the floral border stripe, cut:
• (2) (2) strips 8" x 127" (8" x 127") lengthwise, parallel to the selvage edge, with the border motif aligned with the edges of the strips
• (2) (2) strips 8" x 110" (8" x 127") lengthwise, parallel to the selvage edge, with the border motif aligned with the edges of the strips

From the yellow tonal, cut:
• (3) (3) strips 18⅜" x WOF; recut

(5) (5) 18⅜" squares and (2) (2) 9⅜" x 9⅜" squares. Cut each 18⅜" square diagonally in half twice to make (18) (20) F triangles. Cut each 9⅜" square diagonally in half once to make (4) (4) G triangles.

From the blue floral tonal, cut:
• (11) (12) strips 2½" x WOF for binding

STEP TWO: PIECING THE QUILT TOP

Note: Use a ¼" seam allowance throughout. Sew all pieces with right sides together and raw edges even, using matching thread. Press seams toward the darker fabric unless otherwise noted.

Sewing the Braid Blocks:

1. Sew a pale yellow A strip lengthwise together with a blue damask B strip. Repeat to make a total of 17 (20) strip sets. Crosscut the strip sets into 150 (180) 4½" AB units.

2. Sew a light green C strip lengthwise together with a dark green D strip. Repeat to make a total of 14 (16) strip sets. Crosscut the strip sets into 120 (144) 4½" CD units.

3. Sew the AB and CD units together in rows. Press seams toward the CD units. Sew the rows together to complete one 12½" x 12½" Braid block. Press seams in one direction. Repeat to make a total of 30 (36) blocks.

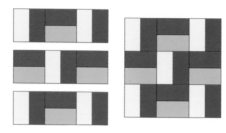

Assembling the Quilt Top:

Note: Refer to the Quilt Assembly Diagram throughout the following steps. Press all border strips away from the quilt center.

1. Arrange the Braid blocks in diagonal rows with the ivory floral E squares and the yellow tonal F triangles.

2. Sew the blocks and pieces together in diagonal rows. Press seams away from the blocks. Sew the rows together, matching all seams.

3. Sew a yellow tonal G triangle to each corner of the quilt center, centering the triangle on the raw edge. Press. Carefully trim the quilt center all the way around, leaving a ¼" seam allowance beyond the block corners, to complete the 85½" x 102½" (102½" x 102½") quilt center.

4. Sew the (10) (10) 1¼" dark green border strips short ends together to make one long strip. Cut two 102½" (102½") strips and two 87" (104") strips. Sew the longer strips to opposite sides of the quilt center and the shorter strips to the top and bottom.

5. Mark the center of each edge of the quilt center. Fold the floral border stripe strips in half to mark the center of each strip. Center the appropriate strip right sides together on each edge and sew to the quilt top, stopping ¼" away from each corner from each corner.

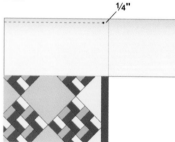

6. Miter the corners, carefully matching the stripe motifs at the ends of each strip and sewing from the outer edge of the border to the quilt corner. Trim the excess fabric leaving a ½" seam allowance. Press corner seams open and border seams toward the border strips to complete the quilt top.

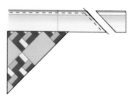

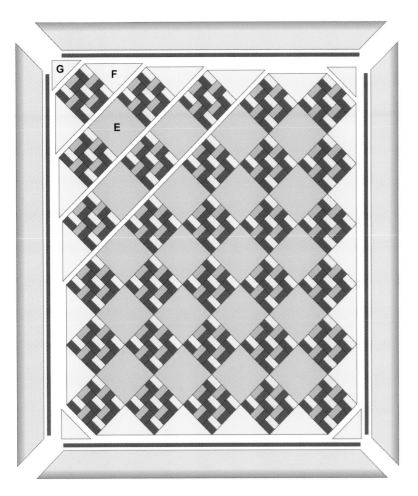

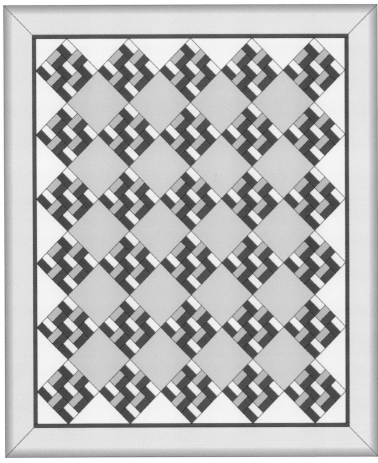

Quilt Assembly Diagram

Alternate Size Quilt Assembly Diagram

STEP THREE:
QUILTING & FINISHING

1. Layer the backing right side down, batting and quilt top right side up. Baste the layers of the quilt together and quilt as desired.

2. Trim the backing and batting even with the quilt top.

3. Sew the short ends of the 2½" x WOF blue floral tonal binding strips together into one long strip. Press the strip in half lengthwise with the wrong sides together. Pin the raw edges of the binding even with the raw edges of the quilt. Sew the binding to the top with a scant ¼" seam allowance. Join the ends of the binding carefully. Turn the binding to the back and hand stitch in place with matching thread and small, nearly invisible stitches.

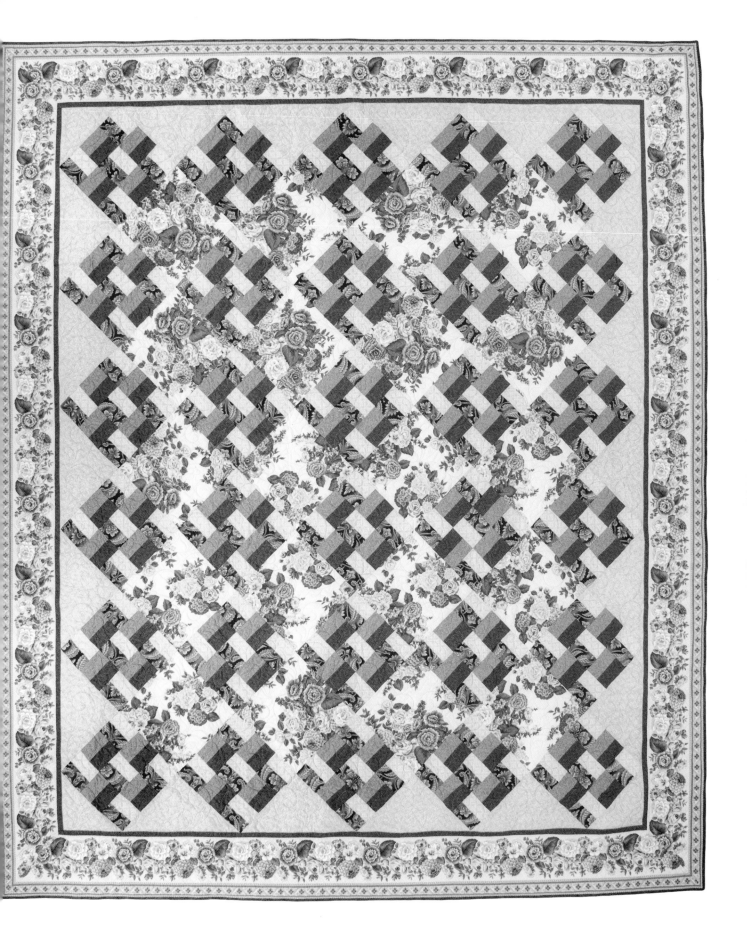

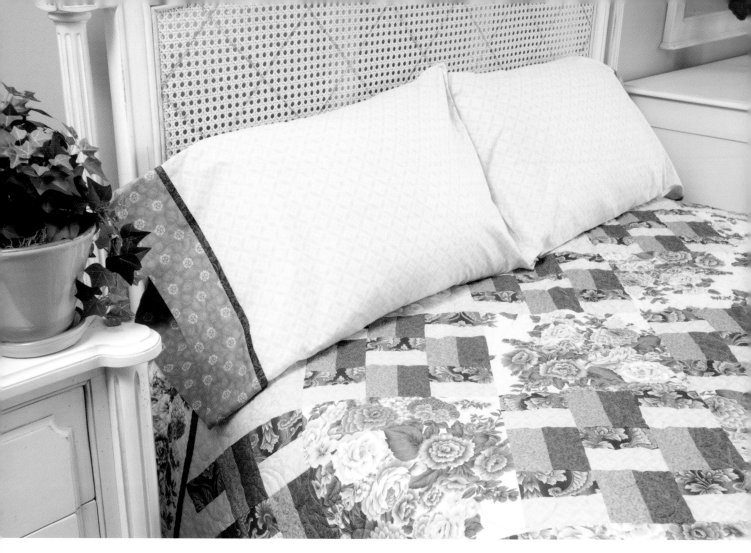

Coordinating Pillowcases

Make a matching set of pillowcases to continue the style of your quilt design.
Add appliqué or a decorative trim to create another design element.

STEP ONE: CUTTING DIRECTIONS

From the main body fabric, cut:
- (2) 31" x 41" rectangles

From the coordinating band fabric, cut:
- (2) 9" x 41" strips

From the accent strip fabric, cut:
- (2) 2" x 41" strips

Fabric & Supply Requirements

- Main body fabric   1⅞ yards
- Coordinating band fabric   ⅔ yard
- Accent strip fabric   ¼ yard
- Sewing thread in colors to match fabrics
- Two queen-size pillows
- Basic sewing supplies & rotary cutting tools

Finished Pillowcase Size: Queen • **Number of Pillowcases:** 2
Skill Level: Beginner

STEP TWO:
SEWING THE PILLOWCASES

Note: Use a ½" seam allowance throughout unless otherwise noted. Sew all pieces with right sides together and raw edges aligned.

1. Press the accent strips in half lengthwise with wrong sides together.

2. Place a folded strip right sides together on one long edge of a coordinating band strip, aligning raw edges. Baste in place ¼" from the raw edges.

3. Place a main body rectangle right sides together on the band strip with raw edges aligned and the accent strip between the layers. Sew together with a ½" seam allowance. Press the seam allowance toward the band strip.

4. Fold the pieced unit in half lengthwise with right sides together, aligning the band and accent strips on each half. Sew along the end of the body and along the side edge of the body/band. Serge or zigzag along the raw edges of the seam allowance to prevent fraying.

5. Turn the raw edge of the band strip ¼" to the wrong side and press. Fold the band strip to the wrong side to cover the seam allowance between the body and the band. Pin in place.

6. Turn the pieced unit right side out. Sew directly in the seam between the body and the band all around to complete one pillowcase. Press.

7. Repeat steps 2–6 to complete a second pillowcase.

Promenade

Dress it up with this fancy floral, a Carolina Lily! Need a small wall hanging over a hall table or your china buffet? Promenade is up to the occasion. Minimal appliqué makes this quilter friendly!

STEP ONE:
CUTTING DIRECTIONS

Note: Please read all directions before cutting fabric. WOF = width of fabric from selvage to selvage, approximately 42". Label the pieces with the letters given in the cutting steps.

From the cream/pink toile, cut:

- (1) strip 5¾" x WOF; recut (5) 5¾" A squares and (1) 2" x 4¼" G rectangle
- (1) strip 2" x WOF; recut (9) 2" x 4¼" G rectangles
- (1) strip 2⅞" x WOF; recut (5) 2⅞" B squares
- (1) strip 3⅛" x WOF; recut (8) 3⅛" squares. Cut each square diagonally in half twice to make (30) D triangles.
- (2) strips 2⅜" x WOF; recut into (15) 2⅜" C squares and (16) 2⅜" I squares. Cut each I square diagonally in half once to make (32) I triangles.
- (1) strip 3½" x WOF; recut into (4) 3½" H squares and (8) 2" M squares

Fabric & Supply Requirements

- Cream/pink toile · ⅞ yard
- Burgundy textured tonal · ⅓ yard
- Lavender textured tonal · ¾ yard
- Green textured tonal · 1 yard
- Deep wine textured tonal · ¼ yard
- Pink textured tonal · ¼ yard
- Burgundy floral · 1 yard
- Backing & Batting · 52" x 52"
- Sewing thread in colors to match fabrics
- Quilting thread in colors to match fabrics
- ⅜" bias bar
- Basic sewing supplies & rotary cutting tools

If you prewash your fabrics, there may be shrinkage. Adjust the yardages accordingly.

Finished Quilt Size: 43¾" x 43¾"   ·   **Finished Block Sizes:** 9" and 6"
Skill Level: Intermediate

From the burgundy textured tonal, cut:

- (1) strip 4⅝" x WOF; recut (8) 4⅝" squares. Cut each square diagonally in half once to make (15) F triangles.
- (1) strip 2⅜" x WOF; recut (8) 2⅜" squares. Cut each square diagonally in half once to make (16) J triangles.

From the lavender textured tonal, cut:

- (1) strip 3⅛" x WOF; recut (8) 3⅛" squares. Cut each square diagonally in half twice to make (30) E triangles.
- (1) strip 2⅜" x WOF; recut (8) 2⅜" squares. Cut each square diagonally in half once to make (16) K triangles.

STEP TWO:
PIECING THE QUILT TOP

Note: Use a ¼" seam allowance throughout. Sew all pieces with right sides together and raw edges even, using matching thread. Press seams toward the darker fabric unless otherwise noted.

Sewing the Carolina Lily Blocks:

1. Fold each bias strip in half lengthwise with wrong sides together and long raw edges aligned. Stitch along the long edge. Insert the bias bar into one strip and press the seam allowance open with the seam centered on one side.

2. Cut five 8½" lengths and ten 2" lengths from the bias strips for stems.

3. Trace and cut 10 leaves from the green textured tonal using the pattern given on page 40. Add a ¼" seam allowance all around the leaf when cutting it out. Turn the seam allowances under all around each leaf shape.

4. To make one Carolina Lily block, fold a toile A square in half diagonally and crease. Place an 8½" stem along the creased centerline. Pin in place. Trim the ends of the stem even with the corners of the square. Insert one end of a 2" stem under the edge of the center stem 2" from the corner of the square. Curve the short stem to the outside edge of the square 2⅛" from the corner. Pin in place. Repeat with a second 2" stem on the other edge of the center stem.

- (1) strip 1½" x WOF; recut (12) 1½" N squares
- (5) strips 2½" x WOF for binding

From the green textured tonal, cut:
- (1) strip 15⅜" x WOF; recut (1) 15⅜" P square, (2) 8⅝" Q squares and (8) 2" L squares. Cut each P square diagonally in half twice to make (4) P triangles and the Q squares diagonally in half once to make (4) Q triangles.
- 1⅜" wide bias strips to total 70"

From the deep wine textured tonal, cut:
- (4) strips 1½" x WOF; recut (16) 9½" O strips

From the pink textured tonal, cut:
- (2) strips 1½" x 30¼" for borders
- (2) strips 1½" x 32¼" for borders

From the burgundy floral, cut:
- (4) strips 6½" x 32¼" for borders

5. Draw a diagonal line on the wrong side of each toile B square. Place a square right sides together on the bottom corner of the A square. Stitch on the marked line. Trim seam allowance to ¼". Press the corner triangle to the right side.

6. Pin a leaf shape 2" up from the corner triangle on each side of the center stem. Appliqué the leaves and stems in place by hand or machine to complete the stem unit.

7. Sew a lavender E triangle to a toile D triangle to make a DE unit. Repeat to make a total of three DE units and three reversed DE units.

Make 3   Reversed
             Make 3

8. Sew a DE unit to one side and a reversed DE unit to an adjacent side of a C square. Press seams toward the DE units. Sew a burgundy F triangle to the DE side on the pieced unit to complete one flower unit. Press seam toward the F triangle. Repeat to make a total of three flower units.

Make 3

9. Sew a toile G rectangle to one side of a flower unit. Press seam toward the G rectangle. Sew this unit to one side of the stem unit. Press seam toward the flower unit. Sew a G rectangle between the two remaining flower units. Press seams toward the G rectangle. Sew this strip to the stem unit to complete one 9½" x 9½" block. Press seam toward the flower unit strip.

10. Repeat steps 4–9 to complete a total of five Carolina Lily blocks.

Sewing the Corner Blocks:

1. To make one Corner block, sew a toile I triangle to a burgundy J triangle. Repeat to make a total of four IJ units. Sew a toile I triangle to a lavender K triangle. Repeat to make a total of four IK units. Sew an IJ unit to an IK unit to make a side strip. Repeat to make a second side strip and two reversed side strips.

Make 4   Make 4   Make 2   Reversed
                              Make 2

2. Sew a side strip to two opposite sides of a toile H square. Press seams toward the H square. Sew a green L square to one end and a toile M square to the remaining end of the reversed side strips. Press seams toward the squares. Sew these strips to the remaining sides of the H square to complete one 6½" x 6½" block. Press seams toward the strips.

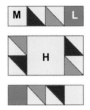

3. Repeat steps 1 and 2 to make a total of four Corner blocks.

Assembling the Quilt Top:
Note: Refer to the Quilt Assembly Diagram throughout the following steps. Press all border strips away from the quilt center.

1. Arrange the Carolina Lily blocks in diagonal block rows with the deep wine O strips and green P triangles. Join the blocks, strips and triangles in rows. Press seams toward the O strips.

2. Arrange the remaining deep wine O strips and lavender N squares in diagonal sashing rows. Join the O and N pieces in rows. Press seams toward the O strips.

3. Sew the block rows together with the sashing rows and add a green Q triangle to each corner. Press seams toward the sashing rows. Carefully trim all the way around, leaving a ¼" seam allowance beyond the corners of the lavender N squares, to complete the 30¼" x 30¼" quilt center.

4. Sew the 1½" x 30¼" pink textured tonal strips to the top and bottom and the 1½" x 32¼" strips to the sides of the quilt center.

5. Sew a 6½" x 32¼" burgundy floral to opposite sides of the quilt center. Sew a Corner block to each end of the remaining 6½" x 32¼" burgundy floral strips. Press seams toward the strips. Sew these strips to the top and bottom of the quilt center to complete the quilt top.

STEP THREE: QUILTING & FINISHING

1. Layer the backing right side down, batting and quilt top right side up. Baste the layers of the quilt together and quilt as desired. Trim the backing and batting even with the quilt top.

2. Sew the short ends of the lavender 2½" x WOF binding strips together into one long strip. Press the strip in half lengthwise with wrong sides together. Pin the raw edges of the binding even with the raw edges of the quilt. Sew the binding to the top with a scant ¼" seam allowance. Join the ends of the binding carefully. Turn the binding to the back and hand stitch with matching thread and small, nearly invisible stitches.

Leaf
Cut 10 from green textured tonal

Quilt Assembly Diagram

Island Breeze

Travel to a tropical isle or venture to the water's edge of a cool mountain lake with Island Breeze. For this project mostly tonals and basics were chosen to give a less frilly look, great for those who don't like flowers.

Fabric & Supply Requirements

	Quilt	Shams (2)
• Medium green tonal	2⅛ yards	⅓ yard
• Light blue textured tonal	½ yard	----
• Deep teal textured tonal	1⅜ yards	⅝ yard
• Gold textured tonal	⅓ yard	----
• Red textured tonal	⅔ yard	----
• Light green textured tonal	⅝ yard	----
• Dark green textured tonal	3 yards	----
• Pale yellow geometric	2⅓ yards	¼ yard
• Plum textured tonal	⅔ yard	----
• Medium teal geometric	1¾ yards	¼ yard
• Blue damask	3¾ yards	2¼ yards
• Backing & Batting	104" x 118"	----

• Sewing thread in colors to match fabrics
• Quilting thread in colors to match fabrics
• 2 queen pillows for shams
• Basic sewing supplies & rotary cutting tools

If you prewash your fabrics, there may be shrinkage. Adjust the yardages accordingly.

Finished Quilt Size: 95¼" x 108¼" • **Finished Sham Size:** 29½" x 20
Finished Block Sizes: 10" and 8" • **Skill Level:** Intermediate

STEP ONE:
CUTTING DIRECTIONS

Note: Please read all directions before cutting fabric. WOF = Width of fabric from selvage to selvage, approximately 42". Label the pieces with the letters given in the cutting steps.

From the medium green tonal, cut:

• (1) strip 3⅜" x WOF; recut (4) 3⅜" squares. Cut each square diagonally in half once to make (8) J triangles.

• (1) strip 2⅞" x WOF; recut (4) 2⅞" squares. Cut each square diagonally in half once to make (8) G triangles.

• (6) strips 10½" x WOF; recut (18) 10½" K squares.

• Shams: (1) strip 6⅝" x WOF; recut (4) 6⅝" squares. Cut each square diagonally in half once to make (8) P triangles.

From the light blue textured tonal, cut:

• (3) strips 2⅛" x WOF; recut (42) 2⅛" squares. Cut each square diagonally in half once to make (84) D triangles.

• (1) strip 4⅝" x WOF; recut (6) 4⅝" squares. Cut each square

diagonally in half once to make (12) B triangles.

From the deep teal textured tonal, cut:

• (3) strips 2⅛" x WOF; recut (42) 2⅛" squares. Cut each square diagonally in half once to make (84) D triangles.

• (1) strip 4⅝" x WOF; recut (6) 4⅝" squares. Cut each square

diagonally in half once to make (12) B triangles.

• (1) strip 3⅜" x WOF; recut (4) 3⅜" squares. Cut each square diagonally in half once to make (8) J triangles.

• (1) strip 2⅞" x WOF; recut (4) 2⅞" squares. Cut each square diagonally in half once to make (8) G triangles.

• (1) strip 8" x WOF; recut (2) 8"

squares. Cut each square diagonally in half once to make (4) M triangles.
- (8) strips 2¼" x WOF for the first border

- Shams: (1) strip 4⅞" x WOF; recut (4) 4⅞" squares. Cut the squares diagonally in half once to make (8) O triangles.
- Shams: (2) strips 3½" x WOF; recut (4) 3½" x 14½" S strips
- Shams: (2) strips 1¾" x WOF; recut (4) 1¾" x 16" R strips

From the gold textured tonal, cut:
- (1) strip 3⅜" x WOF; recut (4) 3⅜" squares. Cut each square diagonally in half once to make (8) J triangles.
- (1) strip 2⅞" x WOF; recut (4) 2⅞" squares. Cut each square diagonally in half once to make (8) G triangles.

From the red textured tonal, cut:
- (3) strips 2⅛" x WOF; recut (42) 2⅛" squares. Cut each square diagonally in half once to make (84) D triangles.
- (1) strip 4⅝" x WOF; recut (6) 4⅝" squares. Cut each square diagonally in half once to make

(12) B triangles.
- (1) strip 3⅜" x WOF; recut (4) 3⅜" squares. Cut each square diagonally in half once to make (8) J triangles.
- (1) strip 2⅞" x WOF; recut (4) 2⅞" squares. Cut each square diagonally in half once to make (8) G triangles.

From the light green textured tonal, cut:
- (2) strips 2⅛" x WOF; recut (28) 2⅛" squares. Cut each square diagonally in half once to make (56) D triangles.
- (1) strip 4⅝" x WOF; recut (4) 4⅝" squares. Cut each square diagonally in half once to make (8) B triangles.
- (1) strip 3⅜" x WOF; recut (4) 3⅜" squares. Cut each square diagonally in half once to make (8) J triangles.
- (1) strip 2⅛" x WOF; recut (4) 2⅛" squares. Cut each square diagonally in half once to make (8) G triangles.

From the dark green textured tonal, cut:
- (4) strips 2⅛" x WOF; recut (70) 2⅛" squares. Cut each square

diagonally in half once to make (140) D triangles.
- (2) strips 4⅝" x WOF; recut (10) 4⅝" squares. Cut each square diagonally in half once to make (20) B triangles.
- (1) strip 4½" x WOF; recut (4) 4½" E squares
- (2) strips 2⅞" x WOF; recut (24) 2⅞" squares. Cut each square diagonally in half once to make (48) F triangles.
- (3) strips 15⅜" x WOF; recut (5) 15⅜" squares. Cut each square diagonally in half twice to make (18) L triangles.
- (9) strips 3" x WOF for the second border

From the pale yellow geometric, cut:
- (7) strips 4⅝" x WOF; recut (56) 4⅝" squares. Cut each square diagonally in half to make (112) A triangles.
- (21) strips 2⅛" x WOF; recut (392) 2⅛" squares. Cut each square diagonally in half once to make (784) C triangles.

- Shams: (1) strip 4⅞" x WOF; recut (4) 4⅞" squares. Cut each square diagonally in half once to make (8) N triangles.

From the plum textured tonal, cut:
- (3) strips 2⅛" x WOF; recut (42) 2⅛" squares. Cut each square diagonally in half once to make (84) D triangles.
- (1) strip 4⅝" x WOF; recut (6) 4⅝" squares. Cut each square diagonally in half once to make (12) B triangles.
- (1) strip 3⅜" x WOF; recut (4) 3⅜" squares. Cut each square diagonally in half once to make

(8) J triangles.
- (1) strip 2⅛" x WOF; recut (4) 2⅞" squares. Cut each square diagonally in half once to make (8) G triangles.

From the medium teal geometric, cut:
- (2) strips 3⅜" x WOF; recut (24) 3⅜" squares. Cut each square diagonally in half once to make (48) I triangles.
- (4) strips 2⅛" x WOF; recut (70) 2⅛" squares. Cut each square diagonally in half once to make (140) D triangles.
- (2) strips 4⅝" x WOF; recut (10) 4⅝" squares. Cut each square diagonally in half once to make (20) B triangles.
- (1) strip 5½" x WOF; recut (4) 5½" H squares
- (11) strips 2½" x WOF for binding

- Shams: (2) strips 2½" x WOF; recut (4) 2½" x 12" Q strips

From the blue damask, cut:
- (4) strips 8½" x WOF for the outer top and bottom borders.
- (2) strips 8½" x 93¾" lengthwise, parallel to the selvage edge, with the border motif centered in each strip
- (6) strips 2⅛" x remaining WOF; recut (56) 2⅛" squares. Cut each square diagonally in half once to make (112) D triangles.
- (1) strip 4⅝" x remaining WOF; recut (8) 4⅝" squares. Cut each square diagonally in half once to make (16) B triangles.

- Shams: (3) strips 20½" x WOF; recut (4) 19¾" x 20½" backing pieces and (4) 4½" x 20½" U strips lengthwise, parallel to the selvage edge
- Shams: (4) 3½" x 22" T strips

STEP TWO:
PIECING THE QUILT TOP
Note: Use a ¼" seam allowance throughout. Sew all pieces with right sides together and raw edges even, using matching thread. Press seams toward the darker fabric unless otherwise noted.

Sewing the Blade Blocks:

1. To make one Blade block, select four plum B triangles and 28 plum D triangles.

2. Sew a yellow A triangle to a plum B triangle to make an AB unit. Repeat to make a total of four AB units. Sew a yellow C triangle to a plum D triangle to make a CD unit. Repeat to make a total of 28 CD units.

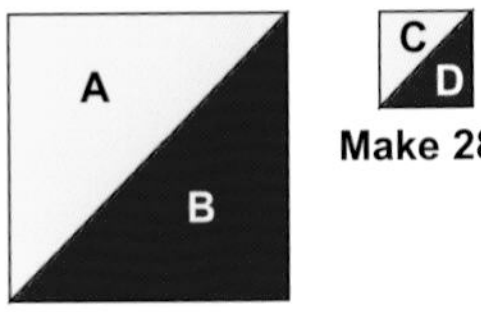

Make 28

Make 4

3. Sew three CD units together to make a strip. Press seams toward the plum triangles. Repeat to make a total of four short strips. Sew four CD units together to make a strip. Press seams toward the plum triangles. Repeat to make a total of four long strips.

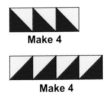

Make 4

Make 4

4. Sew a short strip to one plum side of each AB unit and a long strip to the remaining plum side to complete four block corners. Press seams toward the strips.

5. Sew the block corners together to complete one 10½" x 10½" Blade block. Press seams.

Make 28

6. Repeat steps 1–5 to complete a total of 28 blocks, using the same color B and D triangles in each block.

Sewing the Wild Goose Chase Center and Corner Blocks:

1. To make one Wild Goose Chase Center block, select two J triangles of each color (light green, medium green, gold, deep teal, red and plum), 12 medium teal I triangles, and one medium teal H square.

2. Sew an I triangle to each J triangle to make 12 IJ units. Press seams toward the I triangles. Sew two same-fabric IJ units together to make a flying geese unit. Press seam to one side. Repeat to make a total of six flying geese units.

3. Sew a red flying geese unit to a plum flying geese unit. Press seam toward the plum unit. Sew this strip to one side of the H square. Press seam toward the H square.

4. Sew a light green flying geese unit to a medium green unit to a gold unit to a deep teal unit to make

a strip. Press seams toward the deep teal end. Sew this strip to the H unit to complete one 10½" x 10½" block. Press seam toward the H square side.

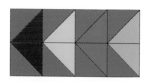

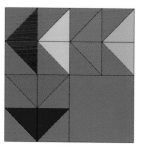

Make 4

5. Repeat steps 1–4 to complete a total of four Wild Goose Chase Center blocks.

6. Repeat steps 1-4 with dark green E squares and F triangles and light green, medium green, gold, deep teal, red and plum G triangles to make four 8½" x 8½" Wild Goose Chase Corner blocks.

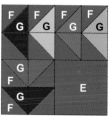

Make 4

Assembling the Quilt Top:
Note: Refer to the Quilt Assembly Diagram throughout the following steps. Press all border strips away from the quilt center.

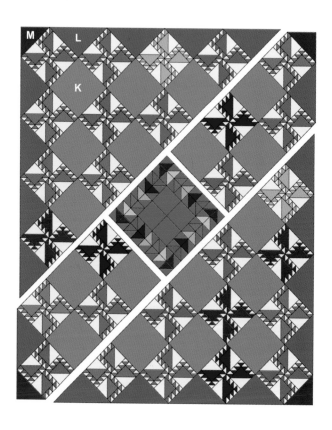

1. Arrange the Blade and Wild Goose Chase Center blocks in diagonal rows with the medium green K squares and the dark green L triangles. Take a moment to study the diagram on page 46 and notice how the Wild Goose Chase Center blocks are arranged to form a center medallion. The blocks are turned so that the medium teal H squares meet in the center.

2. Join the blocks, squares and triangles together in diagonal rows, alternating the color placement of the Blade blocks as desired. Press seams toward the K squares and L triangles.

3. Sew the block rows together to form five sections, carefully matching seams. Press seams toward the K squares.

4. Sew the sections together, matching all seams, and add a deep teal M triangle to each corner. Press. Carefully trim all the way around, leaving a ¼" seam allowance beyond the block corners, to complete the 71¼" x 85¼" quilt center.

5. Sew the deep teal 2¼" x WOF strips short ends together to make one long strip. Cut two 85¼" strips and two 74¾" strips. Sew the longer strips to the long sides of the quilt center and the shorter strips to the top and bottom.

6. Sew the dark green 3" x WOF strips short ends together to make one long strip. Cut two 88¾" strips and two 79¾" strips. Sew the longer strips to the long sides of the quilt center and the shorter strips to the top and bottom.

7. Sew the blue damask 8½" x 93¾" strips to the long sides of the quilt center. Sew the blue damask 8½" x WOF strips short ends together to make one long strip, carefully matching the fabric print at the ends of the strips. Cut two 79¾" strips. Sew a Wild Goose Chase Corner square to each end of these strips, taking care to orient the direction of the fabric print and the blocks. Press seams toward the strips. Sew these pieced strips to the top and bottom of the quilt center to complete the quilt top.

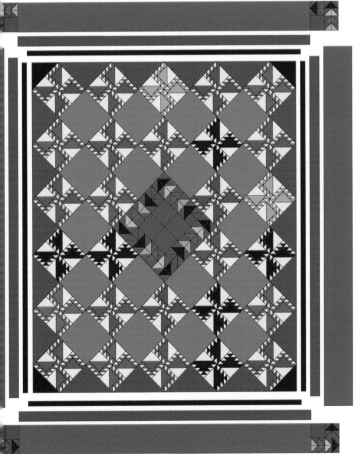

Quilt Assembly Diagram

STEP THREE:
QUILTING & FINISHING

1. Layer the backing right side down, batting and quilt top right side up. Baste the layers of the quilt together and quilt as desired. Trim the backing and batting even with the quilt top.

2. Sew the short ends of the medium teal 2½" x WOF binding strips together into one long strip. Press the strip in half lengthwise with wrong sides together. Pin the raw edges of the binding even with the raw edges of the quilt. Sew the binding to the top with a scant ¼" seam allowance. Join the ends of the binding carefully. Turn the binding to the back and hand stitch with matching thread and small, nearly invisible stitches.

STEP FOUR:
COMPLETING THE SHAMS

Note: *Press all seams away from the sham center. Refer to the Sham Assembly Diagram throughout the following steps.*

1. To make the Pinwheel blocks, sew a pale yellow N triangle to a deep teal O triangle. Press seam toward the deep teal. Repeat to make a total of eight NO units. Sew two units together to make a row. Press seam to the deep teal side. Repeat to make a total of four rows. Join two rows to complete one 8½" x 8½" block. Repeat to make a second block. Press.

Make 2

2. Sew a medium green P triangle to each side of the Pinwheel blocks to make the sham centers. Press seams toward the triangles.

3. Sew a medium teal Q strip to the sides of each center.

4. Sew a deep teal R strip to the top and bottom and a deep teal S strip to the sides of each center.

5. Sew a blue damask T strip to the top and bottom and a blue damask U strip to the sides of each center to complete the sham tops.

Hint

If you wish to quilt the sham, now is the time to do it. Layer a 39" x 29" piece of batting and muslin and quilt as desired.

6. Complete the shams referring to the instructions on page 27.

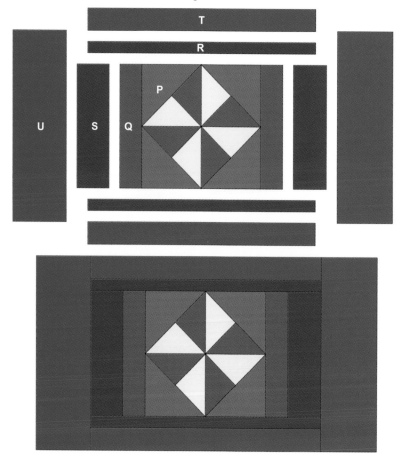

Sham Assembly Diagram

Monterey Sunrise

Wake up to sunshine! This pretty, lighthearted quilt adds a bit of sunshine wherever it goes. Whether you choose to use it as a wall hanging, lap quilt or table topper in your breakfast nook, this smile maker will soon become a family favorite.

STEP ONE:
CUTTING DIRECTIONS

Note: Please read all directions before cutting fabric. WOF = width of fabric from selvage to selvage, approximately 42". Label the pieces with the letters given in the cutting steps.

From the cream tonal, cut:
- (1) strip 2⅞" x WOF; recut (9) 2⅞" A squares and (4) 2½" C squares. Cut each A square diagonally in half once to make (18) A triangles.
- (1) strip 5¼" x WOF; recut (5) 5¼" squares. Cut each square diagonally in half twice to make (18) D triangles.
- (1) strip 4⅞" x WOF; recut (5) 4⅞" squares. Cut each square diagonally in half once to make (9) K triangles.
- (3) strips 2½" x WOF; recut (18) 2½" x 6½" I rectangles
- (1) strip 2¼" x WOF; recut (10) 2¼" squares. Cut each square diagonally in half once to make (20) O triangles.

From the dark green textured tonal, cut:
- (2) strips 2⅞" x WOF; recut (18) 2⅞" squares. Cut each square

Fabric & Supply Requirements

- Cream tonal — ⅞ yard
- Dark green textured tonal — ⅜ yard
- Light green textured tonal — ¼ yard
- Medium blue geometric — ⅓ yard
- Pink textured tonal — ¼ yard
- Peach textured tonal — ⅔ yard
- Light blue textured tonal — ¼ yard
- Dark blue textured tonal — 1⅓ yards
- Cream floral — 1⅜ yards
- Backing & Batting — 65" x 65"
- Sewing thread in colors to match fabrics
- Quilting thread in colors to match fabrics
- Basic sewing supplies & rotary cutting tools

If you prewash your fabrics, there may be shrinkage. Adjust the yardages accordingly.

Finished Quilt Size: 56½" x 56½" • **Finished Block Sizes:** 10" and 6"
Skill Level: Intermediate

---

diagonally in half once to make (36) B triangles.
- (1) strip 3⅝" x WOF; recut (2) 3⅝" squares. Cut each square diagonally in half once to make (4) Q triangles.

From the light green textured tonal, cut:
- (1) strip 4⅞" x WOF; recut (5) 4⅞" E squares and (2) 3⅝" R

squares. Cut each square diagonally in half once to make (9) E triangles and (4) R triangles.

From the medium blue geometric, cut:
- (1) strip 4⅞" x WOF; recut (5) 4⅞" squares. Cut each square diagonally in half once to make (9) H triangles.
- (1) strip 2⅞" x WOF; recut (9)

2⅞" squares. Cut each square diagonally in half once to make (18) J triangles.

From the pink textured tonal, cut:
- (1) strip 4⅞" x WOF; recut (5) 4⅞" squares. Cut each square diagonally in half once to make (9) G triangles.

From the peach textured tonal, cut:
- (2) strips 4⅞" x WOF; recut (9) 4⅞" squares. Cut each square diagonally in half once to make (18) F triangles.
- (5) strips 1½" x WOF for first border

From the light blue textured tonal, cut:
- (1) strip 2¼" x WOF; recut (10) 2¼" squares. Cut each square diagonally in half once to make (20) P triangles.

From the dark blue textured tonal, cut:
- (1) strip 3⅞" x WOF; recut (8) 3⅞" squares. Cut each square diagonally in half once to make (16) S triangles.

- (1) strip 15⅜" x WOF; recut (2) 15⅜" squares. Cut each square diagonally in half twice to make (8) M triangles.
- (1) strip 8" x WOF; recut (2) 8" squares. Cut each square diagonally in half once to make (4) N triangles.
- (6) strips 2½" x WOF for binding

From the cream floral, cut:
- (4) strips 6½" x 45" lengthwise, parallel to the selvage edge, for outer border
- (4) 10½" L squares from remaining fabric width

STEP TWO:
PIECING THE QUILT TOP
Note: Use a ¼" seam allowance throughout. Sew all pieces with right sides together and raw edges even, using matching thread. Press seams toward the darker fabric unless otherwise noted.

Sewing the Basket Blocks:

1. To make one Basket block, sew a cream A triangle to a dark green B triangle to make an AB unit.

Repeat to make a second AB unit. Sew a dark green B triangle to a cream D triangle to make a BD unit. Repeat to make a reversed BD unit.

Make 2   Reversed

2. Sew an AB unit to the dark green end of each BD unit. Sew a pieced strip to one short side of a light green E triangle. Press seam toward the E triangle. Sew a cream C square to the AB end of the remaining pieced strip. Press seam toward the C square. Sew this strip to the remaining short side of the E triangle to complete the basket top. Press seam toward the strip.

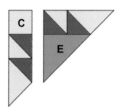

Hint

Apply spray starch to the E and F triangles and press dry to stabilize the long bias edges before stitching them to other pieces.

3. Sew a pink G triangle to a medium blue H triangle. Sew a peach F triangle to each pink side of the pieced unit to complete the basket base.

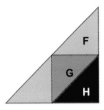

4. Sew the basket base to the basket top. Press seam toward the basket base.

5. Sew a medium blue J triangle to one end of two cream I rectangles. Sew these strips to the basket base edges of the pieced unit. Press seams toward the strips. Sew a cream K triangle to the angled corner to complete one 10½" x 10½" block.

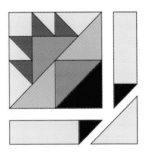

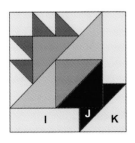

6. Repeat steps 1–5 to complete a total of nine Basket blocks.

Sewing the Corner Blocks:

1. To make one Corner block, sew a cream O triangle to a light blue P triangle to make an OP unit. Repeat to make a total of five OP units. Sew two units together to make a strip. Sew the three remaining units together to make a strip.

2. Sew a dark green Q triangle to a light green R triangle to make a QR unit. Sew the pieced strips from step 1 to the dark green sides of the QR unit to complete the block center. Press seams toward the QR unit.

3. Sew a dark blue S triangle to each side of the block center to complete one 6½" x 6½" block. *Note: The S triangles will overlap more than ¼" at the corners of the center unit. This is correct.*

4. Repeat steps 1–3 to complete a total of 4 Corner blocks.

Assembling the Quilt Top:
Note: Refer to the Quilt Assembly Diagram throughout the following steps. Press all border strips away from the quilt center.

1. Arrange the Basket blocks in diagonal rows with the cream floral L squares and dark blue M triangles.

2. Join the blocks, squares, and triangles together in diagonal rows, alternating the blocks with the L squares. Press seams away from the blocks.

3. Sew the rows together, matching all seams, and add a dark blue N triangle to each corner. Press. Carefully trim all the way around, leaving a ¼" seam allowance beyond the block corners, to complete the 43" x 43" quilt center.

4. Sew the peach 1½" x WOF strips short ends together to make one long strip. Cut two 43" strips and two 45" strips. Sew the shorter strips to the top and bottom and the longer strips to opposite sides of the quilt center.

5. Sew a 6½" x 45" cream floral strip to opposite sides of the quilt center. Press seams toward the strips. Sew a Corner block to each end of the two remaining 6½" x 45" cream floral strips, paying close attention to the positioning of the blocks. Press seams toward the strips. Sew these strips to the top and bottom of the quilt center to complete the quilt top.

STEP THREE:
QUILTING & FINISHING

1. Layer the backing right side down, batting and quilt top right side up. Baste the layers of the quilt together and quilt as desired. Trim the backing and batting even with the quilt top.

2. Sew the short ends of the dark blue 2½" x WOF binding strips together into one long strip. Press the strip in half lengthwise with wrong sides together. Pin the raw edges of the binding even with the raw edges of the quilt. Sew the binding to the top with a scant ¼" seam allowance. Join the ends of the binding carefully. Turn the binding to the back and hand stitch with matching thread and small, nearly invisible stitches.

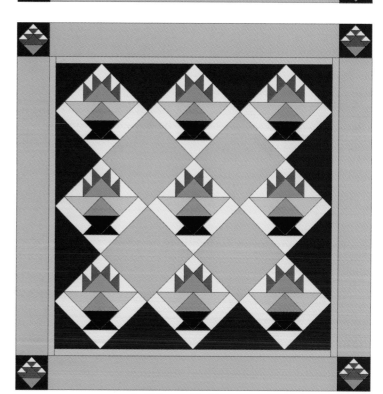

Quilt Assembly Diagram

Cyrpess Rose

In the heat of the day, the coolest place is sometimes found in the shade of the Cypress tree. Lavishly dressed in a bouquet of summer flowers, Cypress Rose will help you find your own retreat!

STEP ONE:
CUTTING DIRECTIONS

Note: Please read all directions before cutting fabric. WOF = Width of fabric from selvage to selvage, approximately 42". Label the pieces with the letters given in the cutting steps. Cutting differences for the alternate size are shown in green.

From the deep wine tonal, cut:
- (2) strips 2⅞" x WOF; recut (16) 2⅞" squares. Cut each square diagonally in half once to make (32) H triangles.
- (4) strips 3⅜" x WOF for second border
- (5) strips 1⅞" x WOF for second border
- (11) strips 2½" x WOF for fourth border

- Shams: (2) strips 3¼" x WOF; recut (4) 14⅝" FF strips
- Shams: (4) strips 2" x 22⅝" for GG

From the burgundy tonal, cut:
- (2) strips 2½" x WOF; recut (28) 2½" F squares
- (2) strips 2⅞" x WOF; recut (16) 2⅞" squares. Cut each square diagonally in half once to make (32) G triangles.

From the pink tonal, cut:
- (2) strips 2½" x WOF; recut (24) 2½" E squares

Fabric & Supply Requirements

	Quilt	Alternate	Shams (2)
• Deep wine tonal	1 yard	1¾ yards	⅝ yard
• Burgundy tonal	½ yard	½ yard	----
• Pink tonal	½ yard	½ yard	----
• Light green textured tonal	3⅞ yards	3⅞ yards	⅓ yard
• Dark green textured tonal	4¼ yards	4¼ yards	⅜ yard
• Rose damask	1⅜ yards	1½ yards	¼ yard
• Burgundy floral	3⅛ yards	6½ yards	2 yards
• Backing & Batting	102" x 119"	116" x 133"	----

- Sewing thread in colors to match fabrics
- Quilting thread in colors to match fabrics
- 2 queen pillows for shams
- Basic sewing supplies & rotary cutting tools

If you prewash your fabrics, there may be shrinkage. Adjust the yardages accordingly.

Finished Quilt Size: 93½" x 110½" (Alternate size 107½" x 124½")
Finished Sham Size: 30⅛" x 20⅛" • **Finished Block Sizes:** 10", 6" and 8½"
Skill Level: Intermediate

- (2) strips 2" x WOF; recut (40) 2" J squares
- (1) strip 3" x WOF; recut (4) 3" R squares

From the light green textured tonal, cut:
- (10) strips 3" x WOF; recut (112) 3" D squares
- (10) strips 6¼" x WOF; recut (28) 6¼" squares. Cut each square diagonally in half twice to make (112) C triangles.
- (25) strips 1¼" x WOF; recut (40) each 1¼" x 2" K, 1¼" x 2¾" L, 1¼" x 3½" M, 1¼" x 4¼" N, 1¼" x 5" O, and 1¼" x 5¾" P

rectangles
- (5) strips 1½" x WOF; recut (4) each 1½" x 3" S, 1½" x 4" T, 1½" x 5" U, 1½" x 6" V, 1½" x 7" W, and 1½" x 8" X rectangles

- Shams: (1) strip 6¼" x WOF; recut (2) 6¼" C squares and (8) 3" D squares. Cut each C square diagonally in half twice to make (8) C triangles.

From the dark green textured tonal, cut:
- (1) strip 2½" x WOF; recut (16) 2½" I squares
- (28) strips 1¼" x WOF; recut (40)

each 1¼" x 2¾" L, 1¼" x 3½" M, 1¼" x 4 ¼" N, 1¼" x 5" O, 1¼" x 5 3/4" P, and 1¼" x 6½" Q rectangles

- (5) strips 1½" x WOF; recut (4) each 1½" x 4" T, 1½" x 5" U, 1½" x 6" V, 1½" x 7" W, 1½" x 8" X, and 1½" x 9" Y rectangles
- (5) strips 10½" x WOF; recut (18) 10½" Z squares
- (3) strips 15⅜" x WOF; recut (5) 15⅜" AA squares and (2) 8" BB squares. Cut each AA square diagonally in half twice to make (18) AA triangles and each BB square diagonally in half once to make (4) BB triangles.

- Shams: (1) strip 8" x WOF; recut (4) 8" squares. Cut each square diagonally in half once to make (8) BB triangles.

From the rose damask, cut:
- (8) strips 2" x WOF for first border
- (11) (12) strips 2½" x WOF for binding

- Shams: (2) strips 1¾" x WOF; recut (4) 14⅝" EE strips

From the burgundy floral, cut:
- (4) strips 5½" x WOF; recut (28) 5½" A squares
- (10) strips 3⅜" x WOF; recut (112) 3⅜" squares. Cut each square diagonally in half once to make (224) B triangles.
- (5) strips 9¾" x WOF; recut (18) 9¾" CC squares. Cut each square diagonally in half twice to make (72) CC triangles.
- (1) strip 5 ⅛" x WOF; recut (8) 5⅛" squares. Cut each square diagonally in half once to make (16) DD triangles.

- (2) strips 5½" x 108", lengthwise, parallel to the selvage edge, for outer top and bottom borders
- (2) strips 5½" x 115", lengthwise, parallel to the selvage edge, for outer side borders

- Shams: (1) strip 5½" x WOF; recut (2) 5½" A squares and (8) 3⅜" B squares. Cut each B square diagonally in half once to make (16) B triangles.
- Shams: (2) strips 19¾" x WOF; recut (4) 19¾" x 20⅝" backing pieces

- Shams: (1) strip 20⅝" x WOF; recut (4) 4½" x 20⅝" HH strips lengthwise, parallel to the selvage edge, and (4) 2" x 22⅝" II strips across the remaining WOF

STEP TWO:
PIECING THE QUILT TOP
Note: Use a ¼" seam allowance throughout. Sew all pieces with right sides together and raw edges even, using matching thread. Press seams toward the darker fabric unless otherwise noted.

Sewing the Sister's Choice Blocks:

1. To make one Sister's Choice block, sew a burgundy F square between two pink E squares to make an E strip. Repeat to make a second E strip. Sew a pink E square between two burgundy F squares to make an F strip. Sew an F strip between two E strips to complete a block center. Press seams toward the E strips. Repeat to make a total of four block centers.

2. Sew a burgundy G triangle to a deep wine H triangle to make a GH unit. Repeat to make a total of eight GH units.

3. Sew a dark green I square between two GH units to make a side strip. Press seams toward the I squares. Repeat to make a total of four side strips.

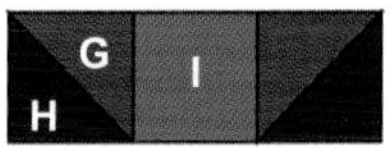

Make 4

4. Sew a side strip to two opposite sides of the block center. Press seams toward the block center. Sew a burgundy F square to each end of one remaining side strip. Press seams toward the F squares. Sew a burgundy F square to one end and a pink E square to the other end of the remaining side strip. Press seams toward the squares. Sew the pieced strips to the remaining sides of the block center to complete one 10½" x 10½" block. Press seams toward the strips.

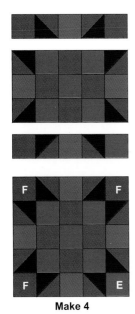
Make 4

5. Repeat steps 1–4 to make a total of four Sister's Choice blocks.

Sewing the Variable Star blocks:

1. To make one Variable Star block, sew a floral B triangle to each angled edge of four light green C triangles to make four BC units. Press seams toward the B triangles.

Make 4

2. Sew a BC unit to two opposite sides of a floral A square. Press seams toward the A square. Sew a light green D square to each end of the remaining BC units. Press seams toward the D squares. Sew a pieced strip to the remaining sides of the A square to complete one 10½" x 10½" block. Press seams toward the strips.

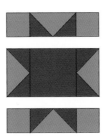

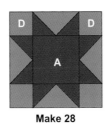
Make 28

3. Repeat steps 1 and 2 to complete a total of 28 Variable Star blocks.

Sewing the Log Cabin blocks:

1. To make one small Log Cabin block, sew a light green K rectangle to one side of a pink J square. Press seam toward the K rectangle.

2. Sew a light green L rectangle to the left edge of the pieced unit. Press seam toward the L rectangle.

3. Sew a dark green L rectangle to the bottom and a dark green M rectangle to the right edge of the pieced unit. Press seams toward the rectangles.

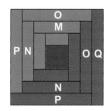

4. Continue to sew light green rectangles to the top and left edges and the dark green rectangles to the bottom and right edges of the pieced unit in alphabetical order to complete one 6½" x 6½" small block. Press seams toward each rectangle.

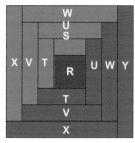

Make 40

5. Repeat steps 1–4 to make a total of (40) 6½" x 6½" small Log Cabin blocks.

6. Repeat steps 1–4 with pink R squares, light green S, T, U, V, W and X rectangles and dark green T, U, V, W, X and Y rectangles to make four 9" x 9" large Log Cabin blocks.

Make 4

Assembling the Quilt Top:
Note: Refer to the Quilt Assembly Diagram throughout the following steps. Press all border strips away from the quilt center unless otherwise instructed.

1. Arrange the Sister's Choice and Variable Star blocks in diagonal rows with the dark green Z squares and AA triangles. Take a moment to study the diagram below to be sure the Sister's Choice blocks are turned so that the pink corner squares meet in the center.

2. Sew the four Sister's Choice blocks together to form the center medallion. Press seams.

3. Join the Variable Star blocks, Z squares and AA triangles together in diagonal rows. Press seams away from the Variable Star blocks.

4. Sew the block rows and center medallion together to form five sections, carefully matching seams. Press seams.

5. Sew the sections together, matching all seams, and add a dark green BB triangle to each corner. Press. Carefully trim all the way around, leaving a ¼" seam allowance beyond the block corners, to complete the 71¼" x 85¼" quilt center.

6. Sew the rose damask 2" x WOF strips short ends together to make one long strip. Cut two 85¼" strips and two 74¼" strips. Sew the longer strips to the long sides of the quilt center and the shorter strips to the top and bottom.

7. Sew the deep wine 1⅞" x WOF strips short ends together to make one long strip. Cut two 80¼" strips and sew to the long sides of the quilt center. Sew the deep wine 3⅜" x WOF strips short ends together to make one long strip. Cut two 77" strips and sew to the top and bottom.

8. Sew a floral CC triangle to two opposite sides of 32 small Log Cabin blocks to make block units. Press seams toward the triangles. Sew a floral CC triangle to one side and two floral DD triangles to two sides of four small Log Cabin blocks to make end units. Press seams toward the triangles. Repeat to make four reversed end units.

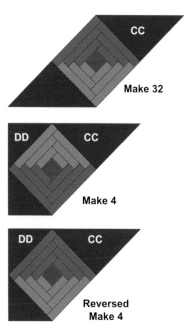

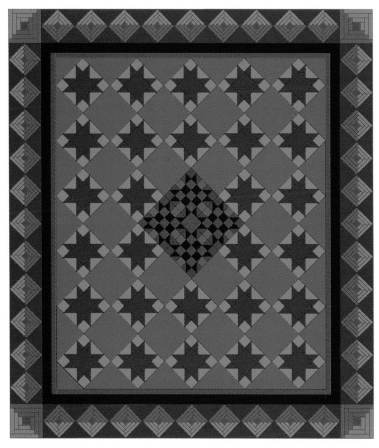

Quilt Assembly Diagram

9. Sew nine block units together with an end unit and reverse end unit to make a side strip. Press seams in one direction. Repeat to make a second side strip. Repeat with seven block units and an end unit and reversed end unit to make two end strips.

10. Sew the side strips to the long sides of the quilt center. Press seams back toward the deep wine border. Sew a large Log Cabin block to the ends of the end strips. Press seams toward the large Log Cabin blocks. Sew these strips to the top and bottom of the quilt center. Press seams toward the strips.

11. For the alternate size, sew the deep wine 2½" x WOF strips short ends together to make one long strip. Cut two 111" strips and two 98" strips. Sew the longer strips to the long sides and the shorter strips to the top and bottom.

12. Sew the 5½" x 115" floral strips to the long sides and the 5½" x 108" floral strips to the top and bottom.

STEP THREE:
QUILTING & FINISHING

1. Layer the backing right side down, batting and quilt top right side up. Baste the layers of the quilt together and quilt as desired. Trim the backing and batting even with the quilt top.

2. Sew the short ends of the rose damask 2½" x WOF binding strips together into one long strip. Press the strip in half lengthwise with wrong sides together. Pin the raw edges of the binding even with the raw edges of the quilt. Sew the binding to the top with a scant ¼" seam allowance. Join the ends of the binding carefully. Turn the binding to the back and hand stitch with matching thread and small, nearly invisible stitches.

Alternate Quilt Assembly Diagram

STEP FOUR:
COMPLETING THE SHAMS

Note: *Press all seams away from the sham center. Refer to the Sham Assembly Diagram throughout the following steps.*

1. Make two Variable Stars blocks referring to Sewing the Variable Star blocks for the quilt.

2. Sew a dark green BB triangle to each side of the Variable Star blocks to complete the sham centers. Press seams toward the triangles.

3. Sew a rose EE strip to two opposite sides of each sham center.

4. Sew a deep wine FF strip to two opposite sides and a deep wine GG strip to the top and bottom of each sham center.

5. Sew a floral HH strip to the top and bottom and a floral II strip to the sides to complete the 30 ⅝" x 20⅝" sham tops.

Hint

If you wish to quilt the sham, now is the time to do it. Layer a 39" x 29" piece of batting and muslin and quilt as desired.

6. Complete the shams referring to the instructions on page 27.

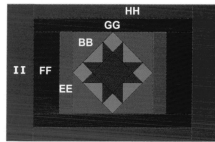

Sham Assembly Diagram

Nantucket Bay

Escape! Wrap yourself in tranquility. In the crisp, cool shades of sparkling water and the warm, earthy colors of the forest, this quilt will be right at home at the beach campfire or in a mountain retreat.

Fabric & Supply Requirements

	Quilt	Alternate	Shams (2)
• Cream/blue toile	1⅞ yards	2¼ yards	¼ yard
• Cream/tan toile	2⅛ yards	2¼ yards	----
• Medium blue geometric	1¼ yards	1¾ yards	----
• Light blue textured tonal	1⅓ yards	1½ yards	⅜ yard
• Dark blue textured tonal	1½ yards	1⅞ yards	⅝ yard
• Black/blue print	¼ yard	¼ yard	⅓ yard
• Light green textured tonal	⅞ yard	1⅛ yards	----
• Dark green textured tonal	⅞ yard	1⅛ yards	----
• Blue damask	¾ yard	⅞ yard	⅓ yard
• Cream damask	2⅞ yards	3¼ yards	1⅞ yards
• Cream vine print	----	----	¼ yard
• Backing & Batting	105" x 105"	118" x 118"	

- Sewing thread in colors to match fabrics
- Quilting thread in colors to match fabrics
- 2 queen pillows for shams
- Basic sewing supplies & rotary cutting tools

If you prewash your fabrics, there may be shrinkage. Adjust the yardages accordingly.

Finished Quilt Size: 96½" x 96½" (Alternate Size: 109¼" x 109¼")
Finished Sham Size: 30¾" x 20¼" • **Finished Block Size:** 9"
Skill Level: Intermediate

STEP ONE:
CUTTING DIRECTIONS

Note: Please read all directions before cutting fabric. WOF = Width of fabric from selvage to selvage, approximately 42". Label the pieces with the letters given in the cutting steps. Cutting for the alternate size is shown in blue.

From the cream/blue toile, cut:

- (2) (2) strips 6⅞" x WOF; recut (10) (12) 6⅞" squares. Cut each square diagonally in half once to make (20) (24) E triangles.

- (2) (2) strips 2" x WOF; recut (28) (32) 2" A squares

- (7) (8) strips 2⅜" x WOF; recut (112) (128) 2⅜" squares Cut each square diagonally in half once to make (224) (256) B triangles.

- (2) (2) strips 3⅞" x WOF; recut (14) (16) 3⅞" squares. Cut each square diagonally in half once to make (28) (32) D triangles.

- (3) (4) strips 6½" x WOF; recut (56) (64) 2" x 6½" C rectangles

- Shams: (1) square 6⅞" x 6⅞". Cut the square diagonally in half once to make (2) E triangles.

From the cream/tan toile, cut:

- (1) (1) strip 6⅞" x WOF; recut (4) (4) 6⅞" squares. Cut each square diagonally in half once to make (8) E triangles.

- (2) (2) strips 14" x WOF; recut (5) (6) 14" squares. Cut each square diagonally in half twice to make (20) (24) R triangles.

- (1) (1) strip 7¼" x WOF; recut (2) (2) 7¼" squares. Cut each square diagonally in half once to make (4) (4) S triangles.

- (10) (11) strips 2½" x WOF for binding

From the medium blue geometric, cut:

- (4) (6) strips 9½" x WOF; recut (13) (21) 9½" Q squares

From the light blue textured tonal, cut:

- (2) (2) strips 2" x WOF; recut (28) (32) 2" G squares
- (4) (4) strips 2⅜" x WOF; recut (56) (64) 2⅜" squares. Cut each square diagonally in half once to make (112) (128) F triangles.
- (2) (2) strips 3⅞" x WOF; recut (14) (16) 3⅞" squares. Cut each square diagonally in half once to make (28) (32) H triangles.
- (2) (2) strips 1⅜" x WOF; recut (20) (32) 1⅜" x 2½" L rectangles
- (3) (4) strips 1⅜" x WOF; recut (20) (32) 1⅜" x 4¼" M rectangles
- (4) (6) strips 1⅜" x WOF; recut (20) (32) 1⅜" x 6" N rectangles
- (4) (7) strips 1⅜" x WOF; recut (20) (32) 1⅜" x 7¾" O rectangles

- Shams: (1) strip 3⅞" x WOF; recut (1) 3⅞" H square, (4) 2⅜" F squares and (2) 2" G squares. Cut each H and F square diagonally in half once to make (2) H triangles and (8) F triangles.
- Shams: (2) strips 2" x WOF; recut (4) 2" x 13¼" U strips

From the dark blue textured tonal, cut:

- (5) (6) strips 2⅜" x WOF; recut (84) (96) 2⅜" squares. Cut each square diagonally in half once to make (168) (192) J triangles.
- (8) (10) strips 2" x WOF; recut (56) (64) 2" x 5⅜" rectangles. Cut (1) end of each rectangle at a 45° angle to make 28 (32) I pieces and 28 (32) reversed I pieces.

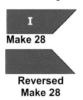

I
Make 28

Reversed
Make 28

- (2) (2) strips 1⅜" x WOF; recut (20) (32) 1⅜" x 2½" L rectangles

- (3) (4) strips 1⅜" x WOF; recut (20) (32) 1⅜" x 4¼" M rectangles
- (4) (6) strips 1⅜" x WOF; recut (20) (32) 1⅜" x 6" N rectangles
- (4) (7) strips 1⅜" x WOF; recut (20) (32) 1⅜" x 7¾" O rectangles

- Shams: (1) strip 2⅜" x WOF; recut (6) 2⅜" J squares and (4) 2" x 5⅜" I rectangles. Cut each J square diagonally in half once to make (12) J triangles. Cut (1) end of each rectangle at a 45° angle to make 2 I pieces and 2 reversed I pieces.
- Shams: (2) strips 3" x WOF; recut (4) 3" x 14¾" X strips
- Shams: (4) strips 1½" x WOF; recut (4) 1½" x 25¼" Y strips

From the black/blue print, cut:

- (2) (2) strips 2½" x WOF; recut (20) (32) 2½" K squares

- Shams: (1) strip 7¼" x WOF; recut (4) 7¼" squares. Cut each square diagonally in half once to make (8) T triangles.

From the light green textured tonal, cut:

- (3) (4) strips 1⅜" x WOF; recut (20) (32) 1⅜" x 4¼" M rectangles
- (4) (6) strips 1⅜" x WOF; recut (20) (32) 1⅜" x 6" N rectangles
- (4) (7) strips 1⅜" x WOF; recut (20) (32) 1⅜" x 7¾" O rectangles
- (5) (7) strips 1⅜" x WOF; recut (20) (32) 1⅜" x 9½" P rectangles

From the dark green textured tonal, cut:

- (3) (4) strips 1⅜" x WOF; recut (20) (32) 1⅜" x 4¼" M rectangles
- (4) (6) strips 1⅜" x WOF; recut (20) (32) 1⅜" x 6" N rectangles
- (4) (7) strips 1⅜" x WOF; recut (20) (32) 1⅜" x 7¾" O rectangles
- (5) (7) strips 1⅜" x WOF; recut (20) (32) 1⅜" x 9½" P rectangles

From the blue damask, cut:

- (8) (9) 2½" x WOF strips for inner border

- Shams: (2) strips 2½" x WOF; recut (4) 2½" x 13¼" V strips
- Shams: (2) strips 1¼" x WOF; recut (4) 1¼" x 20¼" W strips

From the cream damask, cut:

- (2) (2) strips 8½" x 97" (109¾"), lengthwise, parallel to the selvage edge for outer side borders
- (10) (12) strips 8½" across the remaining WOF for outer top and bottom borders

- Shams: (2) strips 3½" x WOF; recut (4) 3½" 16¾" Z strips
- Shams: (4) strips 2½" x WOF; recut (4) 2½" x 31¼" ZZ strips
- Shams: (2) strips 21½" x WOF; recut (4) 19¾" x 21½" backing pieces

From the cream vine print, cut:

- Shams: (1) strip 3⅞" x WOF; recut (1) 3⅞" D square and (8) 2⅜" B squares. Cut each D and B square diagonally in half once to make (2) D triangles and (16) B triangles.

- Shams: (1) strip 2" x WOF; recut (2) 2" A squares and (4) 2" x 6½" C rectangles.

STEP TWO: PIECING THE QUILT TOP

Note: Use a ¼" seam allowance throughout. Sew all pieces with right sides together and raw edges even, using matching thread. Press seams toward the darker fabric unless otherwise noted.

Sewing the Amish Basket Blocks:

1. To make one Amish Basket A block, sew a dark blue J triangle to a cream/blue B triangle to make a BJ unit. Repeat to make a total of 4 units. Repeat with light blue F triangles and cream/blue B triangles to make 4 BF units.

Make 4

Make 4

2. Sew two light blue/cream BF units between two dark blue/cream BJ units to make a side strip. Press seams in one direction. Repeat to make a reversed side strip. Sew a cream/blue A square to one end of the reversed side strip. Press seam toward the square. Sew the side strip and reversed side strip to two adjacent sides of a cream/blue E triangle to complete the basket top. Press seams toward the E triangle.

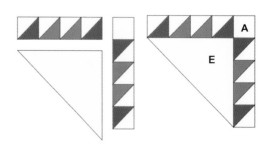

3. Sew a dark blue I piece to one side of a light blue H triangle. Press seam toward the I piece. Sew a light blue G square to a dark blue reverse I piece. Press seam toward the reverse I piece. Sew the two pieced sections together. Press seam toward the GI section to complete the basket bottom. Sew the basket bottom to the basket top; press seam toward the basket top.

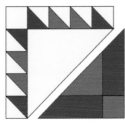

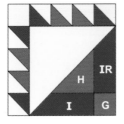

4. Sew a dark blue J triangle to one end of two cream/blue C rectangles to make one CJ unit and one reversed CJ unit. Press seams toward the C rectangles. Sew a CJ unit to one side of the pieced section and a reversed CJ unit to the adjacent side. Press seams toward the CJ units. Add a cream/blue D triangle to the corner of the pieced unit to complete one 9½" x 9½" block. Press seam toward the D triangle.

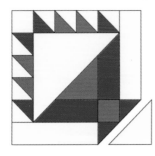

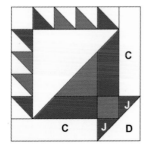

5. Repeat steps 1–4 to make a total of 20 (24) Amish Basket A blocks.

6. To make one Amish Basket B block, repeat steps 1–4 except use a cream/tan E triangle to complete one 9½" x 9½" block. Repeat to make a total of 8 (8) blocks.

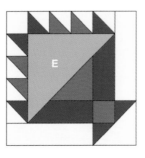

Sewing the Courthouse Steps Blocks:

1. To make one Courthouse Steps block, sew a light blue L rectangle to one side of a black/blue K square and a dark blue L rectangle to the opposite side of the square. Press seams toward the L rectangles.

2. Sew a light green M rectangle to one side of the center unit and a dark green M rectangle to the opposite side. Press seams toward the M rectangles.

3. Sew a light blue M rectangle to the top and a dark blue M rectangle to the bottom of the center unit. Press seams toward the M rectangles.

4. Continue to add light green and dark green rectangles to the sides and light blue and dark blue rectangles to the top and bottom of the center in alphabetical order to complete one 9½" x 9½" Courthouse Steps block. Press all seams away from the block center.

5. Repeat steps 1–4 to make a total of 20 (32) blocks.

Assembling the Quilt Top:

Note: Refer to the Quilt Assembly Diagram throughout the following steps. Press all border strips away from the quilt center unless otherwise instructed.

1. Arrange the blocks in rows with the cream/tan R triangles and S triangles and the medium blue Q squares.

2. Join the blocks, squares and triangles in each row, taking care to orient the basket blocks in the proper directions. Press all seams toward the Courthouse Steps blocks. *Note: The Amish Basket B blocks are used in the quilt center and the Amish Basket A blocks are used around the outside.*

Hint

Make a photocopy of the quilt diagram and mark off each row as you complete it to be sure you are picking up the right blocks for the next row.

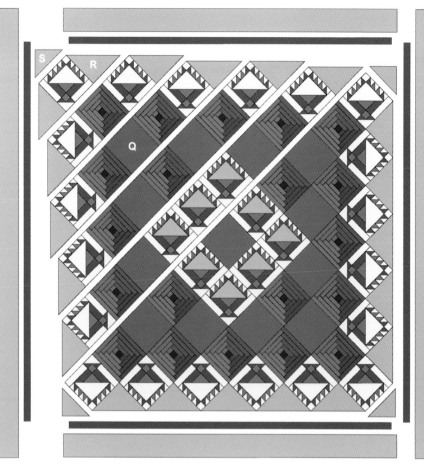

3. Sew the rows together, matching all seams, to complete the 77" x 77" (89¾" x 89¾) quilt center. Press seams in one direction.

4. Sew the blue damask 2 1/2" x WOF strips together on the short ends to make a long strip. Cut two 77" (89¾") strips and two 81" (93¾") strips. Sew the shorter strips to the top and bottom of the quilt center and the longer strips to the remaining sides. Press seams toward the strips.

5. Sew the cream damask 8½" x remaining WOF strips together on the short ends to make a long strip. Cut two 81" (93¾") strips. Sew the strips to the top and bottom of the quilt center. Press seams toward the strips. Sew the cream damask 8½" x 97" (8½" x 109¾") strips to the remaining sides to complete the quilt top. Press seams toward the strips.

STEP THREE:
QUILTING & FINISHING

1. Layer the backing right side down, batting and quilt top right side up. Baste the layers together and quilt as desired.

2. Trim the backing and batting even with the quilt top.

3. Sew the short ends of the 2½" x WOF cream/tan toile binding strips together into one long strip. Press the strip in half lengthwise with wrong sides together. Pin the raw edges of the binding even with the raw edges of the quilt. Sew the binding to the top with a scant ¼" seam allowance. Join the ends of the binding carefully. Turn the binding to the back and hand stitch it in place with matching thread and small, nearly invisible stitches.

Quilt Assembly Diagram

STEP FOUR:
COMPLETING THE SHAMS

Note: *Press all seams away from the sham center. Refer to the Sham Assembly Diagram throughout the following steps.*

1. Make two Amish Basket Blocks referring to steps 1–4 of Sewing the Amish Basket Blocks for the quilt.

2. Sew a black/blue T triangle to each side of the blocks to complete the sham centers. Press seams toward the triangles.

3. Sew a light blue U strip to two opposite sides of each sham center.

4. Sew the blue damask V strips to two opposite sides and the blue damask W strips to the top and bottom of the sham centers.

5. Sew the dark blue X strips to two opposite sides and the dark blue Y strips to the top and bottom of the sham centers.

6. Sew the cream damask Z strips to two opposite sides and the cream damask ZZ strips to the top and bottom of the sham centers to complete the 31¾" x 20¾" sham tops.

Hint

If you wish to quilt the sham, now is the time to do it. Layer the top with a 39" x 29" piece of batting and muslin and quilt as desired.

7. Complete the shams referring to the instructions on page 27.

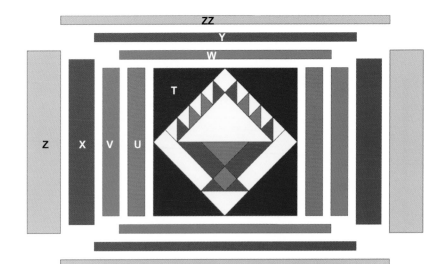

Sham Assembly Diagram

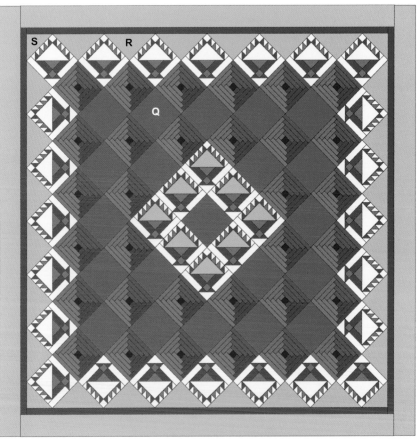

Alternate Quilt Assembly Diagram

Paso Doble Runner

The Paso Doble is a lively style of dance that originated in Southern France and is associated with the dramatic movements of the Spanish Toreador. Choose just the right colors for this project and it will make the perfect accent for any occasion.

STEP ONE:
CUTTING DIRECTIONS

Note: Please read all directions before cutting fabric. WOF = width of fabric from selvage to selvage, approximately 42". Label the pieces with the letters given in the cutting steps.

OPTION 1: BLACK

From the black rosebud print, cut:
- (2) strips 1¼" x WOF for A

From the yellow-green textured tonal, cut:
- (2) strips 1¼" x WOF for C

From the burgundy tonal, cut:
- (2) strips 1¼" x WOF for B

From the green tonal, cut:
- (1) strip 9¾" x WOF; recut (2) 9¾" E squares, (2) 5⅛" F squares and (4) 1¼" G squares. Cut each E square diagonally in half twice to make (8) E triangles and each F square diagonally in half once to make (4) F triangles.
- (4) strips 2¼" x WOF for binding

From the dark purple textured tonal, cut:
- (3) strips 1½" x WOF for borders
- (1) strip 4¼" x WOF' recut (4) 4¼" H squares

Fabric & Supply Requirements

Option 1: Black
• Black rosebud print	¼ yard
• Yellow-green textured tonal	¼ yard
• Burgundy tonal	¼ yard
• Green tonal	¾ yard
• Dark purple textured tonal	½ yard
• Black floral	1⅜ yards
• Backing & Thin Batting	26" x 60"
• Sewing thread in colors to match fabrics	
• Quilting thread in colors to match fabrics	
• Basic sewing supplies & rotary cutting tools	

Option 2: Green
• Medium olive textured tonal	¼ yard
• Light olive tonal	¼ yard
• Cream/tan toile	⅜ yard
• Cream damask	⅜ yard
• Sage green solid	⅝ yard
• Backing & Thin Batting	26" x 43"

If you prewash your fabrics, there may be shrinkage. Adjust the yardages accordingly.

Finished Runner Size: 18" x 52" (Option 2: 18" x 35")
Finished Block Size: 6" • **Skill Level:** Experienced Beginner

From the black floral, cut:
- (2) strips 4¼" x 45" lengthwise, parallel to the selvage edge, for borders
- (2) strips 1¼" x 42" lengthwise, parallel to the selvage edge, for D
- (1) strip 4½" across the remaining WOF; recut (2) 4¼" x 11" for borders

OPTION 2: GREEN

From the medium olive textured tonal, cut:
- (2) strips 1¼" x WOF for A and C

From the light olive tonal, cut:
- (2) strips 1¼" x WOF for B and D

From the cream/tan toile, cut:
- (1) strip 9¾" x WOF; recut (1) 9¾" E square, (2) 5⅛" F squares and (4) 1½" G squares. Cut the E square diagonally in half twice to make (4) E triangles and the F squares diagonally in half once to make (4) F triangles.

From the cream damask, cut:
- (2) strips 4¼" x WOF; recut (2) 28" strips and (2) 11" strips for borders

From the sage green solid, cut:
- (2) strips 1½" x WOF; recut (2) 26" strips and (2) 9" strips for borders
- (1) strip 4¼" x WOF; recut (4) 4¼" H squares
- (3) strips 2½" x WOF for binding

STEP TWO:
PIECING THE RUNNER TOP

Note: Use a ¼" seam allowance throughout. Sew all pieces with right sides together and raw edges even, using matching thread. Press seams toward the darker fabric unless otherwise noted. Information for Option 2 is shown in green.

Sewing the Rail Fence Blocks:

1. Sew the A, B, C and D 1¼" x WOF strips lengthwise together to make a strip set. Press seams in one direction. Repeat to make a second strip set for Option 1. Crosscut the strip sets into (20) (12) 3½" segments.

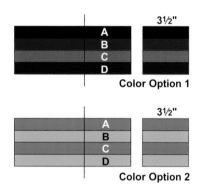

Color Option 1

Color Option 2

2. Sew four segments together to make one 6½" x 6½" Rail Fence block. Repeat to make a total of five (three) blocks.

Color Option 1
Make 5

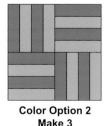

Color Option 2
Make 3

Assembling the Runner Top:

Note: Refer to the Runner Assembly Diagram on page 76 throughout the following steps. Press all border strips away from the runner center.

1. Arrange the blocks with the E and F triangles (see diagrams on page 76). Sew the blocks and triangles together into pieced units as arranged. Press seams away from the blocks. Join the units to complete the 9" x 43" (9" x 26") runner center. Press seams in one direction.

2. For Option 1, sew the 1½" x WOF dark purple strips short ends together to make a long strip. Cut into two 43" strips and two 9" strips. Sew the longer strips to the long sides of the runner center. Press seams toward the strips. Sew a G square to each end of the shorter strips. Press seams toward the strips. Sew these strips to the ends of the runner center. (For Option 2, follow step 2 instructions except use the 1½" x 26" and 1½" x 9" sage green border strips.)

3. For Option 1, sew the 4¼" x 45" black floral strips to the long sides of the runner center. Press seams toward the strips. Sew an H square to each end of the 4¼" x 11" black floral strips. Press seams toward the strips. Sew these strips to the ends of the runner center to complete the top. (For Option 2, follow step 3 instructions except use the 4¼" x 28" and 4¼" x 11" cream damask border strips.)

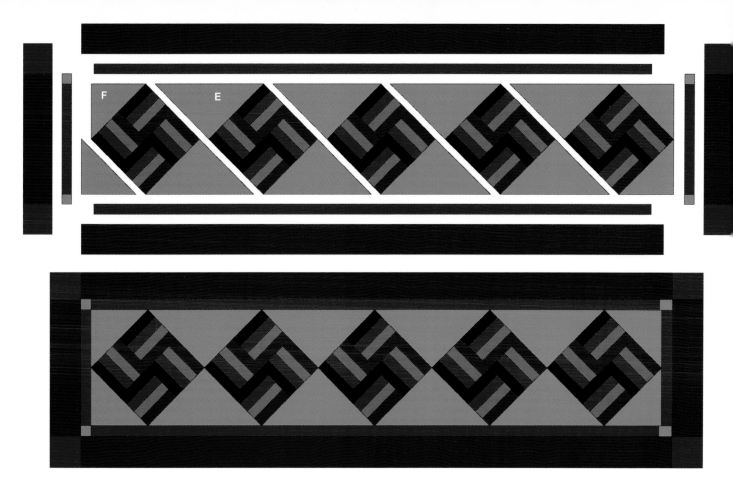

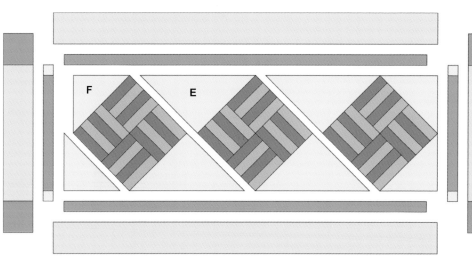

Option 1 Runner Assembly Diagram

STEP THREE:
QUILTING & FINISHING

1. Layer the backing right side down, batting and runner top right side up. Baste the layers of the runner together and quilt as desired. Trim the backing and batting even with the runner top.

2. Sew the short ends of the green tonal (sage green solid) 2½" x WOF binding strips together into one long strip. Press the strip in half lengthwise with wrong sides together. Pin the raw edges of the binding even with the raw edges of the runner. Sew the binding to the top with a scant ¼" seam allowance. Join the ends of the binding carefully. Turn the binding to the back and hand stitch with matching thread and small, nearly invisible stitches.

Option 2 Runner Assembly Diagram

Paso Doble Placemats

Complete your table décor with a set of two placemats to
match the shorter Paso Doble runner.

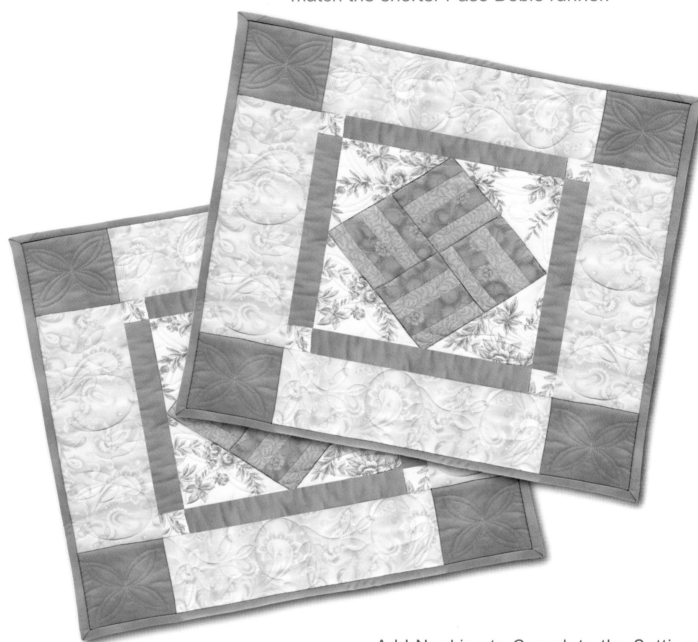

Add Napkins to Complete the Setting

Purchase ⅝ yard of fabric for each 18"-square napkin.

- Cut (2) 19" x 19" fabric squares.
- Place the squares right sides together.
- Stitch around the outside with a ½" seam allowance, leaving a 3" opening on one side.
- Clip the corners close to the line of stitching.
- Turn right side out through the opening.
- Turn the opening edges in ½" and press the edges flat.
- Hand stitch the opening closed.
- Stitch ¼" from the edge all around to complete the napkin.

STEP ONE:
CUTTING DIRECTIONS

From the medium olive textured tonal, cut:
- (2) strips 1¼" x WOF for A and C

From the light olive tonal, cut:
- (2) strips 1¼" x WOF for B and D

From the cream/tan toile, cut:
- (1) strip 5⅛" x WOF; recut (4) 5⅛" F squares and (8) 1½" I squares. Cut the F squares diagonally in half once to make (4) F triangles.

From the cream damask, cut:
- (2) strips 4¼" x WOF; recut (4) 4¼" x 11" J strips
- (2) strips 2¼" x WOF; recut (4) 2¼" x 11" L strips

From the sage green solid, cut:
- (2) strips 1½" x WOF; recut (8) 1½" x 9" H strips
- (1) strip 2¼" x WOF; recut (8) 2¼" x 4¼" K pieces
- (4) strips 2½" x WOF for binding

STEP TWO:
COMPLETING THE PLACEMATS

Note: Press all seams away from the block centers of the placemats.

1. Prepare two Rail Fence blocks referring to the table runner instructions.

2. Sew an F triangle to each side of each block.

3. Sew an H strip to opposite sides of the center units. Sew an I square to each end of the remaining H strips. Sew the pieced strips to the remaining sides of the center units.

4. Sew a J strip to opposite sides of the center units. Sew a K piece to each end of the L strips. Sew the pieced strips to the remaining sides of the center units to complete the 18½" x 14½" runner tops.

5. Quilt and finish the placemats referring to the table runner instructions.

Fabric & Supply Requirements

Medium olive textured tonal	1/4 yard
Light olive tonal	1/4 yard
Cream/tan toile	1/4 yard
Cream damask	1/2 yard
Sage green solid	5/8 yard
Backing & Thin Batting	(2) 26" x 22"

If you prewash your fabrics, there may be shrinkage. Adjust the yardages accordingly.

Finished Placemat Size: 18" x 14" • **Finished Block Size: 6"**

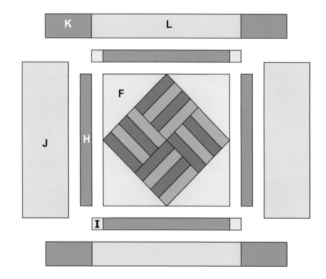

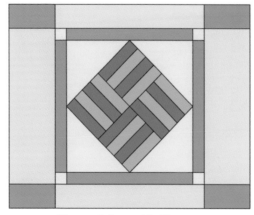

Placemat Assembly Diagram

Mirabelle

Subtle, classic elegance is abundantly evident when toile is mixed with floral motifs. The repetitive use of the toile fabric in the background of the blocks, the setting squares and triangles, and the border strips enhances and accentuates the graphic nature of the block motif. This quilt design is not, however, limited to the use of toile alone. Using a focal fabric, in this case a bouquet floral, creates an equally stunning quilt. For a soft, feminine style, choose light colors and lower contrast fabrics (Color Option 2). For a more dramatic look, choose darker colors and higher contrast accent colors. (Color Option 3)

Fabric & Supply Requirements

	Quilt	Shams (2)
• Green tonal	¾ yard	¼ yard
• Burgundy tonal	1 yard	¼ yard
• Medium purple tonal	1 yard	⅔ yard
• Burgundy floral	1⅔ yards	2 yards
• Medium rose tonal	----	⅓ yard
• Cream/pink toile	9 yards	⅝ yard
• Backing & Batting	112" x 112"	----

- Sewing thread in colors to match fabrics
- Quilting thread in colors to match fabrics
- 2 queen pillows for shams
- Basic sewing supplies & rotary cutting tools

If you prewash your fabrics, there may be shrinkage. Adjust the yardages accordingly.

Finished Quilt Size: 104" x 104" • Finished Sham Size: 30" x 20"
Finished Block Sizes: 9" and 6"
Skill Level: Experienced Beginner

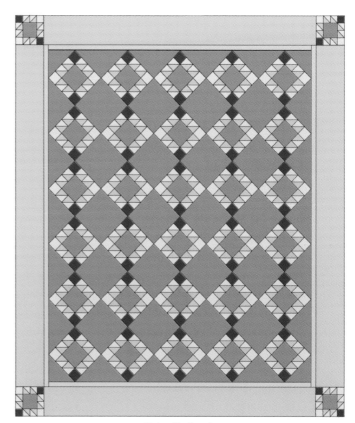

Color Option 2

Color Option 3

STEP ONE:
CUTTING DIRECTIONS

Note: *Please read all directions before cutting fabric. WOF = Width of fabric from selvage to selvage, approximately 42". Label the pieces with the letters given in the cutting steps.*

From the green tonal, cut:
- (7) strips 2¾" x WOF; recut (98) 2¾" E squares
- (1) strip 2" x WOF; recut (4) 2" J squares

- Shams: (4) 2¾" x 2¾" E squares

From the burgundy tonal, cut:
- (8) strips 3⅛" x WOF; recut (98) 3⅛" squares. Cut each square diagonally in half once to make (196) B triangles.
- (1) strip 2⅜" x WOF; recut (8) 2⅜" squares. Cut each square diagonally in half once to make (16) I triangles.
- Shams: (4) 3⅛" x 3⅛" squares. Cut each square diagonally in half once to make (8) B triangles.

From the medium purple tonal, cut:
- (8) strips 3⅛" x WOF; recut (98) 3⅛" squares. Cut each square diagonally in half once to make (196) C triangles.
- (1) strip 2⅜" x WOF; recut (8) 2⅜" squares. Cut each square diagonally in half once to make (16) H triangles.

- Shams: (4) 3⅛" x 3⅛" squares. Cut each square diagonally in half once to make (8) C triangles.
- Shams: (2) strips 3" x WOF; recut (4) 3" x 13¼" R strips

From the burgundy floral, cut:
- (7) strips 5" x WOF; recut (49) 5" F squares
- (9) strips 2" x WOF for the inner border

- Shams: (1) 5" x 5" F square
- Shams: (1) strip 20½" x WOF; recut (4) 4⅞" x 20½" lengthwise, parallel to the selvage edge, and (4) 2½" x 21¾" across the remaining WOF
- Shams: (2) strips 19¾" x WOF; recut (4) 19¾" x 20½" backing pieces

From the medium rose tonal, cut:
- Shams: (1) strip 7¼" x WOF; recut (4) 7¼" squares. Cut each square diagonally in half once to make (8) Q triangles.

From the cream/pink toile, cut:
- (16) strips 3⅛" x WOF; recut (196) 3⅛" squares. Cut each square diagonally in half once to make (392) A triangles.
- (7) strips 2¾" x WOF; recut (98) 2¾" D squares
- (1) strip 2 3/8" x WOF; recut (16) 2 3/8" squares. Cut each square diagonally in half once to make (32) G triangles.
- (1) strip 3½" x WOF; recut (4) 3½" L squares and (8) 2" K squares
- (9) strips 9½" x WOF; recut (36) 9½" M squares
- (2) strips 14" x WOF; recut (6) 14" squares. Cut each square diagonally in half twice to make (24) N triangles.
- (1) strip 7¼" x WOF; recut (2) 7¼" squares. Cut each square diagonally in half once to make (4) O triangles.
- (11) strips 2½" x WOF for binding
- (2) strips 6½" x 92½" lengthwise, parallel to the selvage edge, for the outer side borders
- (7) strips 6½" x remaining WOF for outer top and bottom borders

- Shams: (1) strip 3⅛" x WOF; recut (8) 3⅛" A squares and (4) 2¾" D squares. Cut each A square diagonally in half once to make (16) A triangles.
- Shams: (2) strips 2¼" x WOF; recut (4) 2¼" x 13¼" S strips
- Shams: (4) strips 2⅛" x WOF; recut (4) 2⅛" x 21¾" T strips

STEP TWO:
PIECING THE QUILT TOP

Note: Use a ¼" seam allowance throughout. Sew all pieces with right sides together and raw edges even, using matching thread. Press seams toward the darker fabric unless other noted.

Sewing the Blocks:

1. To make one Center block, sew a toile A triangle to four burgundy B triangles to make AB units. Repeat with A triangles and lavender C triangles to make four AC units.

2. Sew an AB unit to an AC unit to make a strip. Press seam toward the AC unit. Repeat to make a second strip. Sew these strips to opposite sides of a burgundy floral F square. Press seams toward the square.

3. Sew an AB unit to an AC unit to make a strip. Press seam toward the AB unit. Sew a green E square to one end and a toile D square to the remaining end. Press seams toward the squares. Repeat to make a second pieced strip. Sew these strips to the remaining sides of the F square to complete one 9½" x 9½" Center block. Press seams toward the strips.

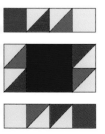 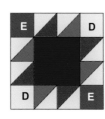

4. Repeat steps 1–3 to complete a total of 49 blocks.

5. Repeat steps 1–3 with toile G triangles and K and L squares, green J squares, medium purple H triangles and burgundy I squares to make four 6½" x 6½" Corner blocks.

Assembling the Quilt Top:
Note: Refer to the Quilt Diagram throughout the following steps. Press all border strips away from the quilt center.

1. Arrange the Center blocks in diagonal rows with the toile M squares and N triangles.

2. Join the blocks, squares and tri- angles together in diagonal rows, al- ternating the blocks with the M squares. Sew the rows together as shown. Press seams toward the M squares and N triangles.

3. Sew the block rows together, matching all seams and adding a toile O triangle to each corner. Press.

Carefully trim all the way around, leaving a ¼" seam allowance beyond the block corners, to complete the 89½" x 89½" quilt center.

4. Sew the burgundy floral 2" x WOF strips short ends together to make one long strip. Cut two 89½" strips and two 92½" strips. Sew the shorter strips to opposite sides and

the longer strips to the top and bot- tom of the quilt center.

5. Sew the toile 6½" x 92½" strips to opposite sides of the quilt center. Sew the 6½" x remaining WOF strips short ends together to make one long strip. Cut to 92½" strips. Sew a Corner block to each end of the strips. Press seams toward the strips. Sew the

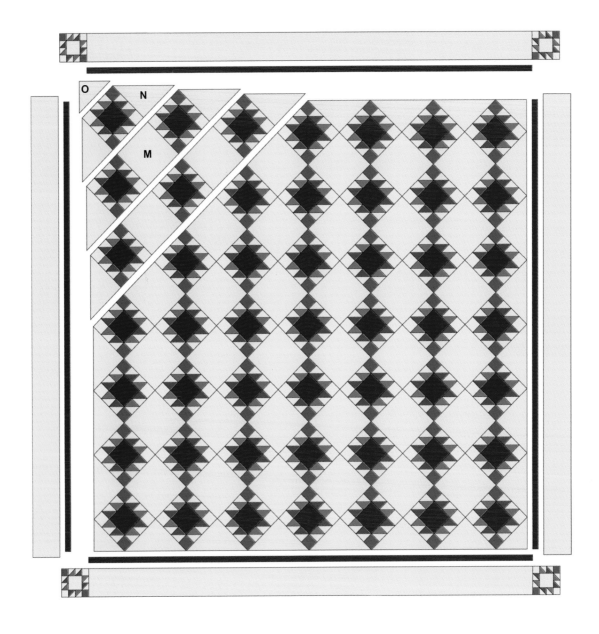

pieced strips to the top and bottom of the quilt center to complete the quilt top.

STEP THREE:
QUILTING & FINISHING

1. Layer the backing right side down, batting and quilt top right side up. Baste the layers of the quilt together and quilt as desired. Trim the backing and batting even with the quilt top.

2. Sew the short ends of the toile 2½" x WOF binding strips together into one long strip. Press the strip in half lengthwise with wrong sides together. Pin the raw edges of the binding even with the raw edges of the quilt. Sew the binding to the top with a scant ¼" seam allowance. Join the ends of the binding carefully. Turn the binding to the back and hand stitch with matching thread and small, nearly invisible stitches.

Quilt Assembly Diagram

STEP FOUR:

COMPLETING THE SHAMS

Note: *Press all seams away from the sham center. Refer to the Sham Assembly Diagram throughout the following steps.*

1. Make two Center blocks referring to steps 1–3 of Sewing the Blocks for the quilt

2. Sew a medium rose Q triangle to each side of the Center blocks to make the sham centers. Press seams toward the triangles.

3. Sew a medium purple R strip to the sides of each center.

4. Sew a toile S strip to the sides of each center and a toile T strip to the top and bottom.

5. Sew a burgundy floral U strip to the top and bottom of each center and a burgundy floral V strip to the sides to complete the sham tops.

Hint

If you wish to quilt the sham, now is the time to do it. Layer a 39" x 29" piece of batting and muslin and quilt as desired.

6. Complete the shams referring to the instructions on page 27.

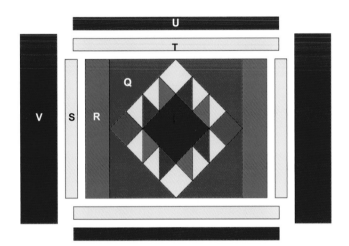

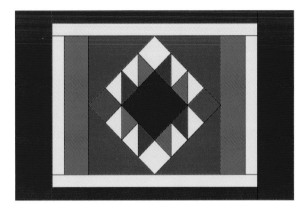

Sham Assembly Diagram

Chantilly

How do you take a very traditional toile and an old-fashioned basket block motif and create a more modern look that sparkles with vivacious color? The surprising element in this quilt is the use of the densely packed floral for the sashing strips. When I auditioned the packed floral, it was as if the quilt had been hit with a myriad of spotlights. The colors used in the blocks "popped." Using the unexpected is often the difference between a nice quilt and a WOW quilt.

STEP ONE:
CUTTING DIRECTIONS

Note: Please read all directions before cutting fabric. WOF = width of fabric from selvage to selvage, approximately 42". Label the pieces with the letters given in the cutting steps.

From the cream/pink toile, cut:
- (2) strips 8 1/2" x 37" for top and bottom borders
- (2) strips 8½" x 53½" lengthwise, parallel to the selvage edge, for side borders
- (2) strips 2⅜" across the remaining WOF; recut (15) 2⅜" squares. Cut each square diagonally in half once to make (30) A triangles.
- (1) strip 3⅞" across the remaining WOF; recut (3) 3⅞" squares. Cut each square diagonally in half once to make (6) I triangles.
- (2) strips 2" across the remaining WOF; recut (12) 2" x 3½" H rectangles
- (2) strips 9¾" across the remaining WOF; recut (3) 9¾" J squares and (2) 5⅛" L squares. Cut each J square diagonally in half twice to make (10) J triangles and the L squares diagonally in half once to make (4) L triangles.

Fabric & Supply Requirements

- Cream/pink toile ... 2⅛ yards
- Cream/tan toile ... ⅔ yard
- Burgundy textured tonal ... 1½ yards
- Lavender textured tonal ... ¼ yard
- Light green textured tonal ... ¼ yard
- Dark green textured tonal ... ⅓ yard
- Pink textured tonal ... ¼ yard
- Burgundy floral ... ⅜ yards
- Backing & Batting ... 61" x 61"
- Sewing thread in colors to match fabrics
- Quilting thread in colors to match fabrics
- Basic sewing supplies & rotary cutting tools

If you prewash your fabrics, there may be shrinkage. Adjust the yardages accordingly.

Finished Quilt Size: 52½" x 53" • **Finished Block Size:** 6"
Skill Level: Intermediate

From the cream/tan toile, cut:
- (1) strip 2⅜" x WOF; recut (15) 2⅜" squares. Cut each square diagonally in half once to make (30) A triangles.
- (1) strip 3⅞" x WOF; recut (3) 3⅞" squares. Cut each square diagonally in half once to make (6) I triangles.
- (1) strip 2" x WOF; recut (12) 2" x 3½" H rectangles
- (1) strip 9¾" x WOF; recut (2) 9¾" K squares and (4) 5⅛" M

squares. Cut each K square diagonally in half twice to make (8) K triangles and each M square diagonally in half once to make (8) M triangles.

From the burgundy textured tonal, cut:
- (2) strips 2⅜" x WOF; recut (18) 2⅜ squares. Cut each square diagonally in half once to make (36) D triangles.
- (2) strips 2" x 34" for top and

bottom borders
- (2) strips 2" x 37½" for side borders
- 2½" wide bias strips to total 300" for binding

From the lavender textured tonal, cut:
- (1) strip 2⅜" x WOF; recut (12) 2⅜" squares. Cut each square diagonally in half once to make (24) C triangles.

From the light green textured tonal, cut:
- (2) strips 2⅜" x WOF; recut (18) 2⅜" squares. Cut each square diagonally in half once to make (36) E triangles.

From the dark green textured tonal, cut:
- (1) strip 2⅜" x WOF; recut (12) 2⅜" squares. Cut each square diagonally in half once to make (24) G triangles.
- (1) strip 3 7/8" x WOF; recut (6) 3⅞" squares. Cut each square diagonally in half once to make (12) F triangles.

From the pink textured tonal, cut:
- (1) strip 2⅜" x WOF; recut (6) 2⅜" squares. Cut each square diagonally in half once to make (12) B triangles.

From the burgundy floral, cut:
- (2) strips 4½" x 34½" for sashing strips

STEP TWO:
PIECING THE QUILT TOP
Note: Use a ¼" seam allowance throughout. Sew all pieces with right sides together and raw edges even, using matching thread. Press seams toward the darker fabric unless otherwise noted.

Sewing the Basket Blocks:

1. To make one pink Basket block, sew a pink toile A triangle to a pink B triangle to make an AB unit. Repeat with two pink toile A triangles and lavender C triangles to make two AC units. Repeat with two pink toile A triangles and burgundy D triangles to make two AD units. Repeat with one light green E triangle and a burgundy D triangle to make one DE unit.

Make 1   Make 2   Make 2   Make 1

2. Sew one each AB, AC and AD units together to make a row. Press seams away from the toile triangles. Sew one each AC and DE units together and add a light green E triangle to the burgundy end to make a row. Press seams toward the light green triangles. Sew a light green E triangle to an AD unit to make a row. Press seam toward the burgundy triangle. Sew the rows together. Press seams in one direction. Add a dark green F triangle to the angled corner to complete the basket top. Press seam toward the F triangle.

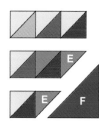

Make 6

3. Sew a dark green G triangle to one end of two pink toile H rectangles to make a GH strip and a reversed GH strip. Sew these strips to two adjacent sides of the basket top. Press seams toward the strips. Sew a pink toile I triangle to the angled G edge to complete one 6½" x 6½" block. Press seam toward the I triangle.

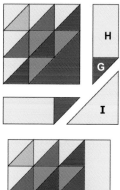

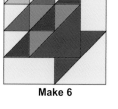
Make 6

4. Repeat steps 1–3 to complete a total of six pink Basket blocks.
5. Repeat steps 1–3 using tan toile A and I triangles and tan toile H rectangles to complete six tan Basket blocks.

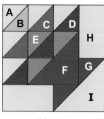
Make 6

Assembling the Quilt Top:

Note: Refer to the Quilt Diagram throughout the following steps. Press all border strips away from the quilt center.

1. Arrange two pink Basket blocks and two tan Basket blocks with four pink toile J triangles, two tan toile K triangles and four tan toile M triangles to make a side block row. Repeat to arrange a second side block row. Repeat with two tan Basket blocks, two pink Basket blocks, four tan toile K triangles, two pink toile J triangles and four pink toile L triangles to make the center block row.

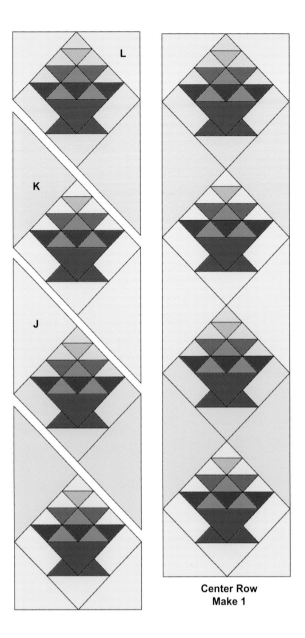

Center Row
Make 1

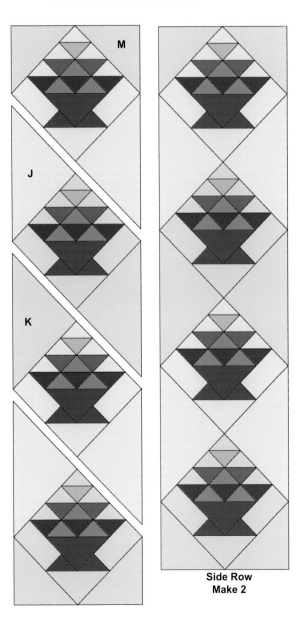

Side Row
Make 2

2. Sew the blocks and triangles together into pieced units as arranged. Press seams away from the blocks. Join the units to complete the row. Press seams in one direction. Repeat to complete the remaining two rows. Each row should measure 9" x 34½".

3. Sew the rows together with the two 4½" x 34½" burgundy floral strips to complete the 34" x 34½" quilt center. Press seams toward the floral strips.

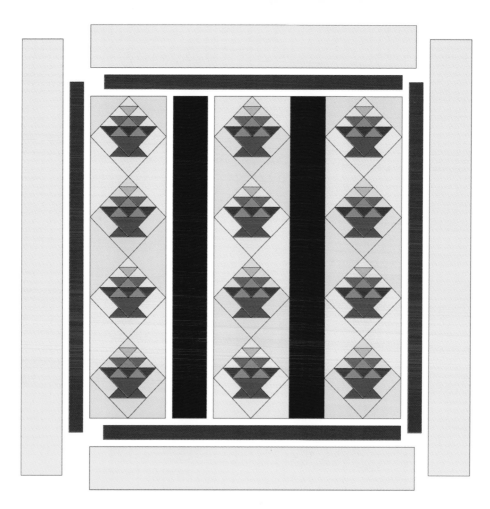

Quilt Assembly Diagram

4. Sew the burgundy textured tonal 2" x 34" strips to the top and bottom and the 2" x 37½" strips to the sides of the quilt center.

5. Sew the cream/pink toile 8½" x 37½" strips to the top and bottom and the 8½" x 53½" strips to the long sides to complete the quilt top.

STEP THREE: QUILTING & FINISHING

1. Layer the backing right side down, batting and quilt top right side up. Baste the layers of the quilt together and quilt as desired. Trim the backing and batting even with the quilt top.

2. Prepare a template for the scallop pattern given on page 94.

3. Fold the quilt in half across the width and mark the center of the side edges with a pin. Fold the quilt in half down the length and mark the center of the top and bottom edges with a pin.

4. Place the scallop template at the pin on one edge of the quilt. Mark around the curved edge of the template. Move the pattern along the edge of the quilt and mark two more scallops. Repeat this on the other side of the pin.

5. Repeat step 4 on each edge of the quilt.

6. Place a dinner plate or a large circle template at each corner of the quilt, matching the edge of the plate or template with the end of the scallop on the two adjacent edges of the quilt. Mark around the plate or template.

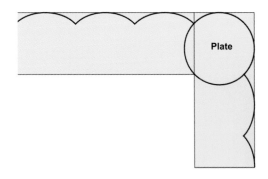

7. Repeat step 6 on each corner of the quilt.

8. Stitch ⅛" inside the marked scallops all the way around the quilt. Do not trim the scallop edge.

9. Sew the short ends of the burgundy 2½" wide bias binding strips together into one long strip. Press the strip in half lengthwise with wrong sides together. Pin the raw edges of the binding even with the marked scallops, making a small pleat at each V and easing, not stretching, the bias around the outer curves. Sew the binding to the top with a scant 1/4" seam allowance. Join the ends of the binding carefully.

10. Carefully trim around the marked scallops.

11. Turn the binding to the back and hand stitch in place with matching thread and small, nearly invisible stitches.

Chantilly Scallop Pattern

Final Step: The Quilt Label

Be sure to add a label to the back of your quilt for future generations. Include the name of the quilt, the maker, your town and state, and the date the quilt was made. If the quilt was made as a gift, include the name of the recipient, your relationship, and the occasion.

Remember that today all of this information is at your fingertips, but tomorrow, generations to come will want to know more about you and your inspiration for making this treasured quilt.

Resources

Marianne Elizabeth's Classically Home
P.O. Box 7166,
Nashua, NH 03060
(603) 880-2021
www.marianneelizabeth.com

RJR Fabrics
2203 Dominguez Street,
Building K-3
Torrance, California 90501
(310) 222-8782
www.rjrfabrics.com

Janet-Lee Santeusanio Woodland Manor Quilting
7 Merchant Rd.
Hampton Falls, NH 03844
603-778-6994
www.woodlandmanorquilting.com

A Stitch In Time
Cathie Shoemaker & Michelle Ryba
978-342-9908
www.astitchintimequilting.com

References

The Quilter's Album of Patchwork Patterns: 4050 Pieced Blocks for Quilters by Jinny Beyer, Breckling Press, 2009

Once More Around the Block by Judy Hopkins, That Patchwork Place, 2003

Fabrics
All projects in this book were made with Marianne Elizabeth's Aubrielle fabric collection.

It wasn't until I became a parent that I realized just how unusual my upbringing was and how it provided me with a framework for thinking. As the daughter of two high school administrators, I had something that very few people have: I was the offspring of two parents with wanderlust. Each year, in addition to the traditional winter break, February recess, spring break, and holiday breaks, my parents had anywhere from 3 weeks to 2 1/2 months of vacation, enabling us to travel the country and, eventually, the world.

After their marriage in 1947, they set out to see the world and create a lifetime of memories. Exploring the United States from coast to coast, before interstate highways, chain eateries, and the Mobil Guide to hotels and restaurants, they saw the less homogenized America in which Americans were people of greater individuality with lifestyles that vary from region to region. Pigeonholed into the back of a car, we sang from coast to coast with the help of the Chevrolet song book and magical invisible lines dividing each sibling from the other. Border disputes are something I am completely conversant in. Diplomacy? Not so much.

As an adult, I have not had the ability to travel for the length of time as I did when growing up. I am so thankful now for the places I've been and the things I've seen. Through travel I became a more inquisitive person. Through travel I enjoyed the beauty of the world and developed an appreciation for the minutia that we often take for granted—the way the light sparkles on the leaves just before the sun sets; the array of colors in the sky when thunderstorms roll across the plains; the fantasy flowers found in the more tropical climes; the silence at a lake's edge just as dawn approaches. The experience of exploring national parks across the United States formed indelible memories. I have recollections of beautiful imagery as seen through the window of our Chevrolet.

Exploring landscapes around the country only helped to foster my love of plants and flowers. Working in a flower shop, with its greenhouse and garden center, helped me to find a place where I felt at home. I still recall the soft fragrance in the greenhouse air early in the morning on a sunshiny day.

But where did my love of fabric come from? My grandmother, a talented seamstress, lived with us and taught me to sew at an early age. She never made quilts, only apparel. Making doll clothes and learning hand embroidery, I loved to play with color and fabric. I loved her sewing box full of skeins and skeins of beautiful DMC colors. Huge fabric stores that offered every type of cloth imaginable were close to home and a favorite outing.

In school I was a student of all things French. I loved the language and learning about the people and culture of the country. I couldn't wait to see the countryside and sit at a café and ride a riverboat down the Seine.

It seems only fitting that these influences—loving the French style and language, an absolute fascination with flowers and plants, and a love of fabric—would lead to becoming a fabric designer. All of these things have been major influences in the fabrics I design.

The Marianne Elizabeth style is about creating comfort and elegance for the "perfect home," the one we all want to come home to. It's taking pretty things and surrounding our world in beauty, long beyond when the flowers fade outdoors. It's giving you a toolbox, the fabric palette, with which to use your imagination and talents to create perfect results: the ones you have made yourself.

May all your quilts be truly loved,

marianne elizabeth